Iowa's
Bicycle
Trails

3rd Edition

An
American Bike Trails
Publication

Iowa's **Bicycle Trails**
3rd Edition

Published by American Bike Trails

Created by Ray Hoven

Designed & Illustrated by Mary C. Rumpsa

Table of Contents

Table of Contents (continued)

Non-Illustrated Trails Listing

Appendices & Indexes

How To Use This Book

This book provides a comprehensive, easy-to-use quick reference to the many off-road trails throughout Iowa. It contains over 100 detailed trail maps, plus overviews covering the state sectionally, organized by east, central and west. Trails are generally grouped alphabetically within Iowa's East, Central and West sections. The sectional overviews are grouped near the front, with a back section cross-referencing counties and towns to trails, and a section listing many of the parks in Iowa with their pertinent information. Each trail map includes such helpful features as location and access, trail facilities, and nearby communities.

Terms Used

Length	Expressed in miles one way. Round trip mileage is normally indicated for loops.
Effort Levels	**Easy** Physical exertion is not strenuous. Climbs and descents as well as technical obstacles are more minimal. Recommended for beginners.
	Moderate Physical exertion is not excessive. Climbs and descents can be challenging. Expect some technical obstacles.
	Difficult Physical exertion is demanding. Climbs and descents require good riding skills. Trail surface may be sandy, loose rock, soft or wet.
Directions	Describes by way of directions and distances, how to get to the trail areas from roads and nearby communities.
Map	Illustrative representation of a geographic area, such as a state, section, forest, park or trail complex.
DNR	Department of Natural Resources
DOT	Department of Transportation

Types of Biking

Mountain	Fat-tired bikes are recommended. Ride may be generally flat but then with a soft, rocky or wet surface.
Leisure	Off-road gentle ride. Surface is generally paved or screened.
Tour	Riding on roads with motorized traffic or on road shoulders.

Riding Tips

- Pushing in gears that are too high can push knees beyond their limits. Avoid extremes by pedaling faster rather than shifting into a higher gear.

- Keeping your elbows bent, changing your hand position frequently and wearing bicycle gloves all help to reduce the numbness or pain in the palm of the hand from long-distance riding.

- Keep you pedal rpms up on an uphill so you have reserve power if you lose speed.

- Stay in a high-gear on a level surface, placing pressure on the pedals and resting on the handle bars and saddle.

- Lower your center of gravity on a long or steep downhill run by using the quick release seat post binder and dropping the saddle height down.

- Brake intermittently on a rough surface.

- Wear proper equipment. Wear a helmet that is approved by the Snell Memorial Foundation or the American National Standards Institute. Look for one of their stickers inside the helmet.

- Use a lower tire inflation pressure for riding on unpaved surfaces. The lower pressure will provide better tire traction and a more comfortable ride.

- Apply your brakes gradually to maintain control on loose gravel or soil.

- Ride only on trails designated for bicycles or in areas where you have the permission of the landowner.

- Be courteous to hikers or horseback riders on the trail, they have the right of way.

- Leave riding trails in the condition you found them. Be sensitive to the environment. Properly dispose of your trash. If you open a gate, close it behind you.

- Don't carry items or attach anything to your bicycle that might hinder your vision or control.

- Don't wear anything that restricts your hearing.

- Don't carry extra clothing where it can hang down and jam in a wheel.

Health Hazards

Hypothermia

Hypothermia is a condition where the core body temperature falls below 90 degrees. This may cause death.

Mild hypothermia

1. Symptoms

    a. Pronounced shivering

    b. Loss of physical coordination

    c. Thinking becomes cloudy

2. Causes

    a. Cold, wet, loss of body heat, wind

3. Treatment

    a. Prevent further heat loss, get out of wet clothing and out of wind. Replace wet clothing with dry.

    b. Help body generate more heat. Refuel with high-energy foods and a hot drink, get moving around, light exercise, or external heat.

Severe Hypothermia

1. Symptoms

    a. Shivering stops, pulse and respiration slows down, speech becomes incoherent.

2. Treatment

    a. Get help immediately.

    b. Don't give food or water.

    c. Don't try to rewarm the victim in the field.

    d. A buildup of toxic wastes and tactic acid accumulates in the blood in the body's extremities. Movement or rough handling will cause a flow of the blood from the extremities to the heart. This polluted blood can send the heart into ventricular fibrillations (heart attack). This may result in death.

    e. Wrap victim in several sleeping bags and insulate from the ground.

Frostbite

Symptoms of frostbite may include red skin with white blotches due to lack of circulation. Rewarm body part gently. Do not immerse in hot water or rub to restore circulation, as both will destroy skin cell.

Heat Exhaustion

Cool, pale, and moist skin, heavy sweating, headache, nausea, dizziness and vomiting. Body temperature nearly normal.

Treatment

Have victim lie in the coolest place available – on back with feet raised. Rub body gently with cool, wet cloth. Give person glass of water every 15 minutes if conscious and can tolerate it. Call for emergency medical assistance.

Heat Stroke

Hot, red skin, shock or unconsciousness; high body temperature.

Treatment

Treat as a life-threatening emergency. Call for emergency medical assistance immediately. Cool victim by any means possible. Cool bath, pour cool water over body, or wrap wet sheets around body. Give nothing by mouth.

Explanation of Symbols

SYMBOL LEGEND

- 🏊 Beach/Swimming
- 🚲 Bicycle Repair
- 🏠 Cabin
- ⚠ Camping
- 🛶 Canoe Launch
- ✚ First Aid
- 🍴 Food
- GC Golf Course
- ? Information
- 🛏 Lodging
- MF Multi-Facilities
- P Parking
- 🪑 Picnic
- 🧍 Ranger Station
- 🚻 Restrooms
- 🏠 Shelter
- T Trailhead/Access
- 🏛 Visitor/Nature Center
- 💧 Water
- 🔭 Overlook/Observation

TRAIL USES LEGEND

- 🚴 Leisure Biking
- 🚵 Mountain Biking
- 🚶 Hiking
- ⛷ Cross-country Skiing
- 🐎 Horseback Riding
- ⛸ Rollerblading
- 🛷 Other

AREA LEGEND

- City, Town
- Parks, Preserves
- Waterway
- Marsh/Wetland
- Mileage Scale
- ★ Points of Interest
- – – County/State
- 🌲 Forest/Woods

TRAIL LEGEND

- ▬▬▬ Bike/Multi Trail
- •••••••• Hiking only Trail
- ▬▬▬ XC Skiing only
- ========== Planned Trail
- ▬ ▬ ▬ ▬ Alternate Trail
- ▬▬▬ Road/Highway
- ┼┼┼┼┼┼ Railroad Tracks

Explanation of Geological Terms

Bog	An acidic wetland that is fed by rainwater and is characterized by open water with a floating mat of vegetation (e.g. sedges, mosses, tamarack) that will often bounce if you jump on it.
Bluff	A high steep bank with a broad, flat, or rounded front.
Canyon	A deep, narrow valley with precipitous sides, often with a stream flowing through it.
Fen	An alkaline wetland that is fed by ground water and is often seen as a wet meadow and characterized by plants like grass or parnasis and sedges that grow in alkaline water.
Forest	A vegetative community dominated by trees and many containing understory layers of smaller trees, shorter shrubs and an herbaceous layers at the ground.
Grove	A small wooded area without underbrush, such as a picnic area.
Herb	A seed producing annual, biennial, or perennial that does not develop persistent woody tissue but dies down at the end of a growing season.
Karst	An irregular limestone region with sinks, underground streams, and caverns.
Lake	A considerable inland body of standing water.
Marsh	A wetland fed by streams and with shallow or deep water. Often characterized by mats of cattail, bulrushes, sedges and wetland forbs.
Mesic	A type of plant that requires a moderate amount of water.
Moraine	Long, irregular hills of glacial till deposited by stagnant and etreating glaciers.
Natural Community	A group of living organisms that live in the same place, e.g. woodland or prairie.

Explanation of Geological Terms (continued)

Park	An area maintained in its natural state as a public property.
Pond	A body of water usually smaller than a lake.
Prairie	Primarily treeless grassland community characterized by full sun and dominated by perennial, native grasses and forbs. Isolated remnants of tall grass prairie can be found along and near the I&M Corridor.
Preserve	An area restricted for the protection and preservation of natural resources.
Ridge	A range of hills or mountains.
Savanna	A grassland ecosystem with scattered trees characterized by native grasses and forbs.
Sedges	Grass-like plants with triangular stems and without showy flowers. Many are dominant in sedge meadows, bogs and fens but others are found in woodlands or prairies.
Shrubs	Low woody plants, usually shorter than trees and with several stems.
Swale	A lower lying or depressed and off wet stretch of land.
Swamp	Spongy land saturated and sometimes partially or intermittently covered with water.
Turf	The upper stratum of soil bound by grass and plant roots into a thick mat.
Wetland	The low lying wet area between higher ridges.

The Iowa Trails Council

The Iowa Trails Council (ITC) is pleased to have participated in the creation of this book. It is our hope that you will find it helpful and that it will provide many days of enjoyment on Iowa's trails.

The Council was founded in 1984. Its purpose is to acquire land for trails, to help develop trails and promote them when completed. It is the only organization in Iowa devoted exclusively to this cause.

The ITC is a not-for-profit membership organization. Its officers and staff are all volunteers working to create more and better trails in Iowa. The ITC publishes a mini-magazine which is distributed to its members in an effort to keep them informed of new and extended trails both inside and outside Iowa, as well as attractions near these trails.

The Council has, since its founding, specialized in acquiring former railroad rights-of-way for conversion to trails. Until very recently Iowa has led the nation in both the number of these rail beds converted and the total mileage, which now amounts to more than 650 miles on 50 former rail corridors. Iowa has consistently maintained its average of approximately 10 percent of the nation's rail-trail conversions.

More often than not these conversions are referred to as bike trails, though they are designed to be multi-purpose. More and more of these are being hard surfaced to satisfy bicyclists and in-line skaters. The ITC initiated the effort to bring the nation's longest trail, coast to coast from California to Delaware, on a 500 mile route across Iowa. Bicyclists are obviously the chief benefactors of the efforts of the Council.

Sandwiched between two of the nation's major rivers, Iowa offers a surprising variety of seasons. The state's rolling terrain can provide both leisurely rides and real outdoor adventure. Many delightful trails can be found in Iowa's state and county parks while other trails act as connectors of these parks or link together metropolitan areas. There are many and various attractions along the way to satisfy most any interest, from museums to covered bridges, from casinos to racing tracks, from fall festivals to movie making sites. No matter where you go we believe you will find friendly faces and the welcome mat will always be out.

New members of the Iowa Trails Council are also most welcome, whether they live inside or outside Iowa. Information may be obtained by writing to the Iowa Trails Council, Post Office Box 131, Center Point, IA, 52213-0131 or by telephoning (319) 849-1844.

Tom F. Neenan
ITC Executive Director

State of Iowa

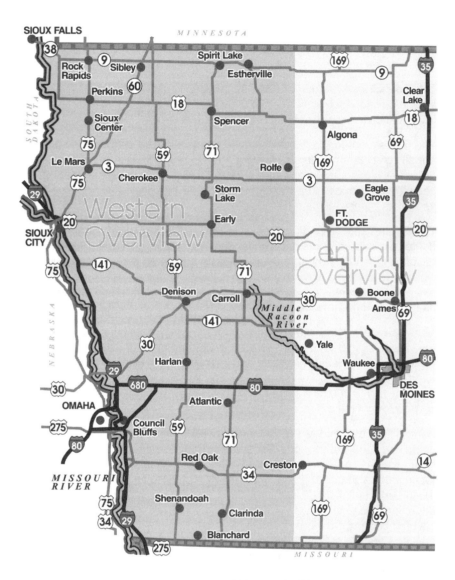

SIOUX FALLS

MINNESOTA

Rock Rapids, Sibley, Perkins, Sioux Center, Le Mars, Cherokee, Spirit Lake, Estherville, Spencer, Algona, Clear Lake, Rolfe, Storm Lake, Early, Eagle Grove, FT. DODGE, Boone, Ames, Denison, Carroll, Yale, Waukee, Harlan, Atlantic, DES MOINES, OMAHA, Council Bluffs, Red Oak, Creston, Shenandoah, Clarinda, Blanchard

SOUTH DAKOTA

NEBRASKA

MISSOURI RIVER

Middle Racoon River

MISSOURI

Western Overview

Central Overview

SIOUX CITY

Shaded Relief Map of the Topographic Surface of Iowa

Courtesy of Iowa Dept. of Transportation

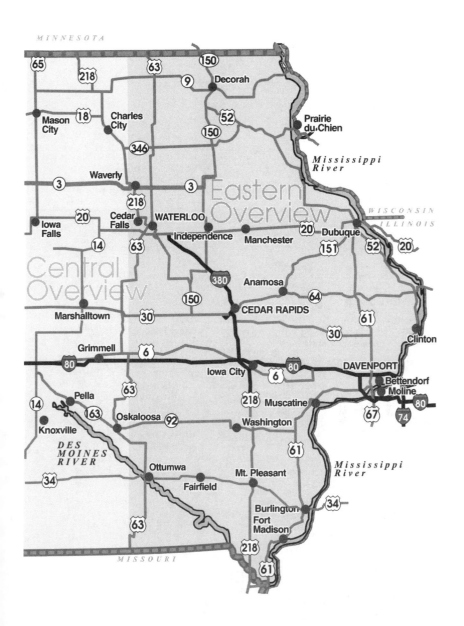

Eastern Iowa Overview

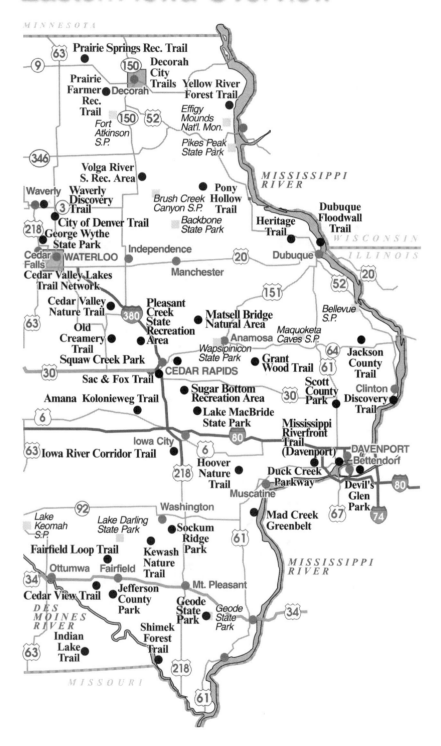

MINNESOTA

Prairie Springs Rec. Trail

(63) (9)

(150) Decorah City Trails

Prairie Farmer Rec. Trail ● Decorah

Yellow River Forest Trail

Fort Atkinson S.P. (150) (52)

Effigy Mounds Nat'l. Mon.

Pikes Peak State Park

MISSISSIPPI RIVER

(346)

Volga River S. Rec. Area ●

Waverly ● Waverly Discovery (3) Trail

Pony Hollow Trail

Brush Creek Canyon S.P.

Backbone State Park

Dubuque Floodwall Trail

Heritage Trail

City of Denver Trail

(218) George Wythe State Park ●

Independence

WATERLOO

Cedar Falls ●

WISCONSIN

ILLINOIS

Dubuque

(20)

Manchester

Cedar Valley Lakes Trail Network

Cedar Valley Nature Trail ●

(63)

Old Creamery Trail ●

Squaw Creek Park

Pleasant Creek State Recreation Area

(380)

Matsell Bridge Natural Area ●

(151)

(52) (20)

Bellevue S.P.

Maquoketa Caves S.P.

Anamosa

Wapsipinicon State Park

(64) Jackson County Trail

(30)

Sac & Fox Trail

CEDAR RAPIDS

Grant Wood Trail (61)

Amana Kolonieweg Trail ●

(6)

Sugar Bottom Recreation Area ●

Lake MacBride State Park ●

Scott County Park (30)

Clinton Discovery Trail ●

(63) Iowa River Corridor Trail ●

Iowa City (6)

(80)

Mississippi Riverfront Trail (Davenport)

DAVENPORT Bettendorf

(218)

Hoover Nature Trail ●

Duck Creek Parkway

Devil's Glen Park

(80)

Muscatine

(74)

Washington

(92)

Mad Creek Greenbelt

(67)

Lake Keomah S.P.

Lake Darling State Park

Sockum Ridge Park

(61)

Fairfield Loop Trail ●

Ottumwa Fairfield

Kewash Nature Trail

MISSISSIPPI RIVER

(34)

Mt. Pleasant ●

Cedar View Trail ●

Jefferson County Park ●

Geode State Park ●

Geode State Park

(34)

DES MOINES RIVER

(63)

Indian Lake Trail ●

Shimek Forest Trail ●

(218)

MISSOURI

(61)

16

Eastern Iowa Trails

Central Iowa Overview

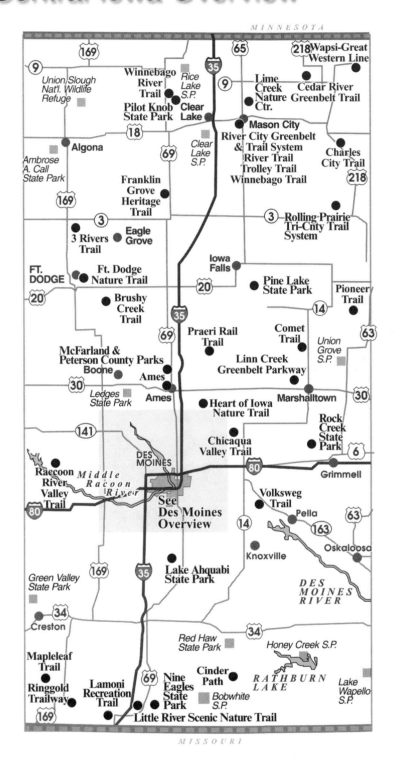

MINNESOTA

(169) (35) (65) (218) Wapsi-Great Western Line

(9)
Union Slough Nat'l. Wildlife Refuge

Winnebago River Trail
Rice Lake S.P.
(9)
Lime Creek Nature Ctr.
Cedar River Greenbelt Trail

Pilot Knob State Park
Clear Lake

(18)
Clear Lake S.P.
(69)

Mason City
River City Greenbelt & Trail System
River Trail
Trolley Trail
Winnebago Trail

Charles City Trail
(218)

Algona
Ambrose A. Call State Park
(169)

Franklin Grove Heritage Trail
(3)

(3) Rolling Prairie Tri-Cnty Trail System

3 Rivers Trail
Eagle Grove

Iowa Falls

FT. DODGE
(20)
Ft. Dodge Nature Trail

Brushy Creek Trail

(20)
Pine Lake State Park
(14)
Pioneer Trail

(35)
(69)
Praeri Rail Trail
Comet Trail
Linn Creek Greenbelt Parkway
Union Grove S.P.
(63)

McFarland & Peterson County Parks
Boone
Ames
(30)
Ledges State Park
Ames

Heart of Iowa Nature Trail
Marshalltown
(30)

Chicaqua Valley Trail
Rock Creek State Park
(6)

(141)
DES MOINES
(80)
Grimmell

Raccoon River Valley Trail
Middle Racoon River
(80)
See Des Moines Overview
Volksweg Trail
Pella
(14)
(163)
(63)

Knoxville
Oskaloosa

Green Valley State Park
(169)
(35)
Lake Ahquabi State Park

DES MOINES RIVER

(34)
Creston

Red Haw State Park
(34)
Honey Creek S.P.

Mapleleaf Trail
Ringgold Trailway
Lamoni Recreation Trail
(69)
Nine Eagles State Park
Cinder Path
Bobwhite S.P.
RATHBURN LAKE
Lake Wapello S.P.

(169)
Little River Scenic Nature Trail

MISSOURI

Des Moines Overview

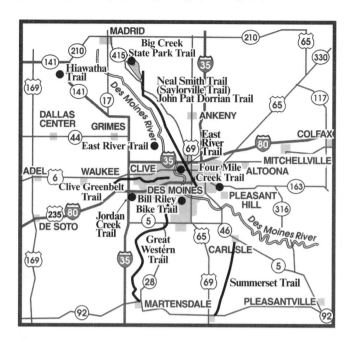

Central Iowa Trails

Western Iowa Overview

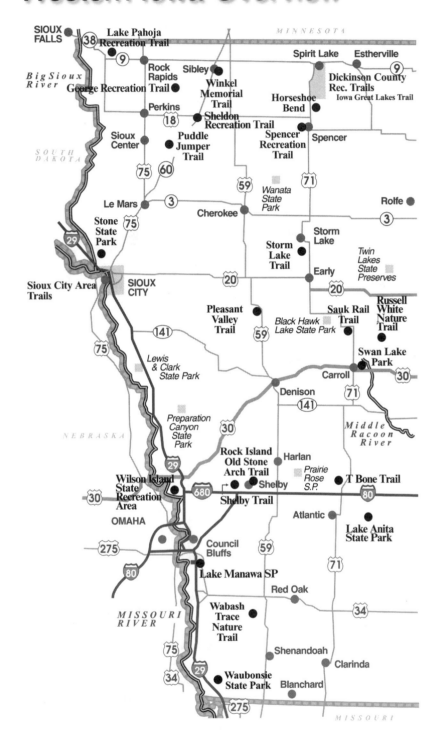

Western Iowa Trails

Stone State Park is one state park hosting a state preserve within its boundaries.

Jerry Leonard

Photo courtesy of Iowa Dept. of Natural Resources

American Discovery Trail

General Overview

The trail is divided into 6 segments totaling 512 miles, mostly existing rail-trails.

Davenport to Cedar Rapids – 97 miles

Cedar Rapids to Waterloo – 62 miles

Waterloo to Marshalltown – 79 miles

Marshalltown to Des Moines – 81 miles

Des Moines to Atlantic – 117 miles

Atlantic to Council Bluffs – 76 miles

Photo courtesy of Iowa Dept. of Tourism

Iowa

Waterloo

Comet Trail

Cedar Valley Nature Trail

Coon Rapids

Marshalltown

Cedar Rapids

Davenport

Melbourne

Hoover Nature Trail

Audubon

Adel

Heart of Iowa Nature Trail

Pioneer Trail

Riverfront Trail

Atlantic

Raccoon River Valley Trail

Muscatine

Des Moines

Council Bluffs

Red Oak

Malvern

Wabash Trace Trail

Affiliated Trails	Riverfront Trail
	Hoover Nature Trail
	Cedar River Trail
	Cedar Valley Nature Trail
	Cedar Valley Lake Trail
	Pioneer Trail
	Comet Trail
	Heart of Iowa Nature Trail
	Saylorville-Des Moines River Trail
	Raccoon River Valley Trail
	T-Bone Trail
	Wabash Trace Trail
	Cedar Lake Trail
	Cedar River Trail
Parks	Deerwood Park
	George Wyth State Park
	Wild Cat Den State Park
	Pleasant Creek State Park

American Discovery Trail (continued)

The American Discovery Trail (ADT) connects with six national scenic trails, 10 national historic trails, 23 national recreational trails and hundreds of local and regional trails. It also connects 14 national parks and 16 national forests. The ADT crosses California, Nevada, Utah, Colorado, Nebraska, Iowa, Illinois, Indiana, Kansas, Missouri, Kentucky, Ohio, West Virginia, Maryland, Washington D.C. and Delaware.

Iowa Section

Davenport to Cedar Rapids
The American Discovery Trail enters Iowa at Davenport, over the recently built ADT Bicycle/Pedestrian Mississippi River Bridge. The route takes you through the downtown area on the Riverfront Trail, which is partly on a rail-with-trail along the Mississippi River. Leaving Davenport, it temporarily follows Hwy 22, through Wildcat Den State Park, to Muscatine, the town where Samuel Clemens (Mark Twain) lived. Turning west, the trail eventually joins the Hoover Nature Trail, a former rail line, at Conesville. Heading north through Nichols and West Liberty, the Hoover Nature Trail passes through West Branch, the birthplace of President Hoover. Continuing north, the Hoover Nature Trail goes through Oasis, Morse, Solon, and Ely and into Cedar Rapids, where the ADT is on the metro trail system.

Cedar Rapids to Waterloo
The American Discovery Trail continues on a paved trail through Hiawatha to the 52 mile long Cedar Valley Nature Trail. This popular and largely paved trail follows the Red Cedar River, passing the faithfully restored Center Point and Gilbertville depots. The northern end of the Cedar Valley Nature Trail is across from Deerwood Park in Evansdale. The Cedar Prairie Trail begins here and takes you into Waterloo, where the Cedar Valley Lakes Trail and trails in George Wyth Memorial State Park becomes the route.

Waterloo to Marshalltown
In the Waterloo-Cedar Falls metro area the American Discovery Trail turns south onto the Sergeant Road Trail to Hudson and then on roads to Voorhies and then west to Reinbeck. From Reinbeck through Morrison to Grundy Center, the ADT continues on the Pioneer Trail, a crushed limestone rail-trail. Again on roads the ADT heads south to Beaman, then turns west and joins the Comet Trail to Conrad, where low traffic roads take you into Marshalltown. There the ADT is on local trails, then back roads going southwest to the Heart of Iowa Trail.

Marshalltown to Des Moines

The Heart of Iowa Trail begins south of Marshalltown at Melbourne, and continues through Rhodes, Collins, and Maxwell, to Slater. From Slater, after a few miles on low traffic roads, the American Discovery Trail meets up with the Saylorville and Neal Smith Trails, which takes you into Des Moines.

Des Moines to Atlantic

West of Des Moines, at Clive, the American Discover Trail becomes part of the Raccoon River Valley Trail, which passes through Waukee, Adel, Redfield, Linden, Panora, and Herndon as it winds through prairie remnants and bottomland timber areas. From there the ADT goes west on Hwy E63, heading to Coon Rapids, there it turns south on Hwy N46. The ADT trail follows Hwy N46 to Hwy F32, heading west into Audubon, there it joins the T-Bone Trail through Hamlin, Exira, and Brayton to Atlantic.

Atlantic to Council Bluffs

From Atlantic, the American Discovery Trail traverses Hwy G30, then M56, through Lewis and Cold Springs State Park, following Hwy 48 to Red Oak. From there it goes west on Hwy 34, through Emerson to Hastings. From Hastings, the ADT goes south on M16 and west on H38 to Malvern, where it joins the Wabash Trace Trail, which takes you through Silver City and Mineola, near the National Park Service's Long Distance Trail Center. At Council Bluffs, it crosses the Missouri River into Nebraska.

Photo courtesy of Iowa Dept. of Tourism

Big Creek State Park

Trail Length	3.5 miles
Surface	Asphalt
Vicinity	Des Moines
Location & Setting	Eleven miles north of Des Moines and seven miles south of Madrid. Enter park area off Hwy. 415 on Beach Drive. Trail runs from Big Creek Beach south, connecting with the Saylorville-Des Moines River Trail for a total of 26 miles.
Information	Iowa Department of Natural Resources (515) 984-6473
County	Polk

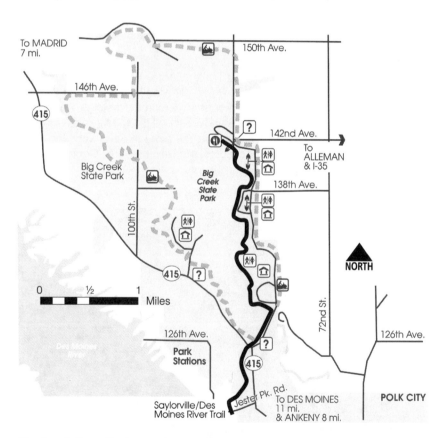

Big Creek State Park contains 3,550 acres with a 866 acre lake. Shelters and picnic area, a beach, two playgrounds and several boat ramps provide a variety of outdoor recreation opportunities. Refreshments are available at the beach during the swimming season.

Bill Riley Trail

Trail Length	1.6 miles, plus over 4 miles of connecting park roads.
Surface	Asphalt
Vicinity	Des Moines
Location & Setting	The north trailhead is located on 45th Street at the Ashworth Pool parking lot. The south trailhead is located at the Water Works Park, 2200 Valley Drive. The trail is flat and winds through Ashworth Park and along the Raccoon River providing great scenery.
Information	Des Moines Park & Recreation (515) 248-6356
County	Polk

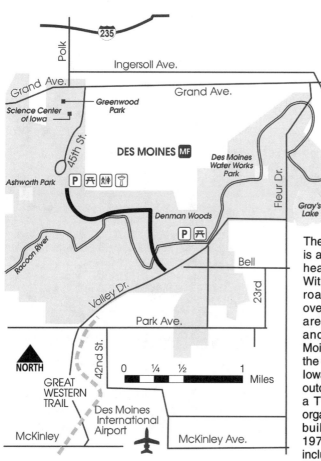

The Bill Riley Bike Trail is a 1.6 mile trail in the heart of Des Moines. With connecting park roads, the length is over 5 miles. Nearby are the water works and Arboretum, Des Moines Art Center and the Science Center of Iowa. Bill Riley was an outdoor enthusiast and a TV personality who organized the effort to build the trail in the 1970's. Future plans include connecting the Bill Riley to the Great Western Trail.

Brushy Creek Recreation Area

Trail Length	50.0 miles, multi-use
Surface	Natural, singletrack
Vicinity	Lehigh, Fort Dodge
Location & Setting	The Brushy Creek State Recreation Area is located five miles northeast of Lehigh on D46 and 15 miles southeast of Fort Dodge - Hwy 20 east to P73 and then south to entrance. It consists of 6500 acres of fields, woodland and stream valley. Winding, smooth singletrack and a few hills.
Information	Brushy Creek State Recreation Area (515) 543-8298
County	Webster

Nearby Attractions

Fort Dodge Blanden Memorial Art Museum The first permanent municipal art gallery constructed in Iowa, located in Oak Hill Historic District. Regional, national and international exhibitions, distinctive collection of American, European and Asian art. Classes, workshops, films, lectures and special events such as the annual Oak Hill Art Festival. Location 920 Third Ave. South.

Fort Museum & Frontier Village 1862 military fort and frontier town, 10 original and replica buildings. Museum collection contains Native American, pioneer and military artifacts from the late 18th century to the present. Relive the area's history at Frontier Days in early June. Location Bus. 20 & Museum Rd.

Brushy Creek State Park

Mark Edwards

Photo courtesy of Iowa Dept. of Natural Resources

Webster City

Kendall Young Library Doll Collection with 170 dolls dating from 1800-1890, Eberle statuettes, American Indian collection. Location 1201 Willson Ave.

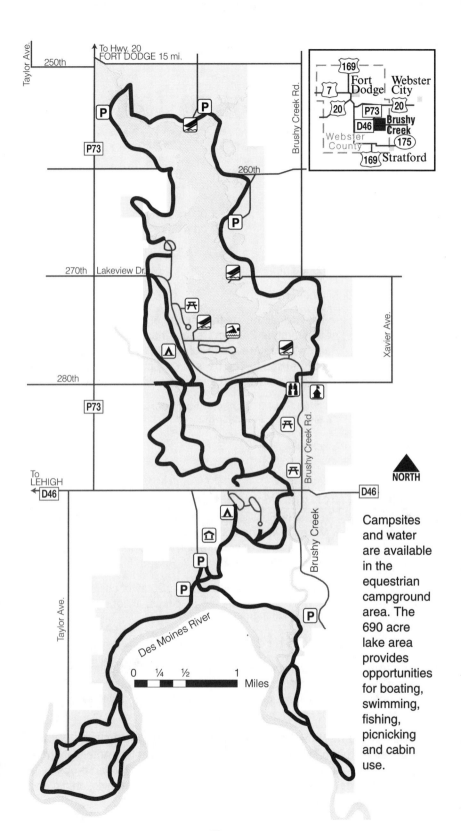

Taylor Ave.

250th

To Hwy. 20
FORT DODGE 15 mi.

P

P

P73

260th

Brushy Creek Rd.

169
Fort
Dodge
7
20
Webster
City
P73
20
D46
**Brushy
Creek**
Webster
County
175
169
Stratford

P

270th   Lakeview Dr.

🏕

🏕

🎇

🏕

🔭

🏛

P73

280th

Xavier Ave.

🏕

To
LEHIGH

D46

🏕

🏠

P

P

D46

Brushy Creek Rd.

Brushy Creek

▲
NORTH

Taylor Ave.

P

Des Moines River

0   ¼   ½   1

Miles

Campsites
and water
are available
in the
equestrian
campground
area. The
690 acre
lake area
provides
opportunities
for boating,
swimming,
fishing,
picnicking
and cabin
use.

Cedar Valley
Harry Cook Nature Trail
Spring Park Connection

Trail Length	Cedar Valley	4.00 miles
	Harry Cook	2.00 miles
	Spring Park	0.75 miles

Surface Crushed stone

Vicinity Mitchell, Osage

Location & Setting In Mitchell, at the southwest end of Cedar River Bridge near interstate Park. In Osage, there are accesses at Falk's Wildlife Area, off Highway 9, at Spring Park and at 1st Street south. The trails largely parallel the Cedar River. The setting is wooded and prairie with rolling scenery.

Information	Mitchell County Conservation Board	(641) 732-5204
	Osage Parks and Recreation	(641) 732-4674

County Mitchell

Nearby Attractions Mason City

Kinney Pioneer Museum Fossils, dolls, ladies' fashions, soda shop. Conastoga wagon, Meredith Wilson collection, one-room school, log cabin, blacksmith shop, horse-drawn farm and fire fighting equipment. Antique cars. Location Municipal Airport entrance Hwy 18 W. Street.

Van Horn's Antique Truck Museum Large display of commercial vehicles from 1908 to 1931, large scale model circus, antique gas pumps, advertising signs. Location Hwy 65 North.

Lime Creek Nature Center 3501 Lime Creek Rd.

Frank Lloyd Wright Stockman House 1908 Prairie School house designed by Frank Lloyd Wright, the only middle-class house of his Prairie School period in the country open to the public. Furnished with Wright-designed furnishings. Location 530 First St. NE.

Charles H. MacNider Museum Tudor-style mansion overlooking Willow Creek features permanent collection of 19th & 20th century American art, the largest collection anywhere of puppets, marionettes and related props by the famous puppeteer Bill Baird. Exhibitions of sculptures, graphics, crafts, and paintings. Location 303 Second St. SE.

A variety of terrain, trees and plants can be observed along the trails. Wildlife consists of many varieties of animals and birds, including fox, hawks, owls, turkeys, egrets, beaver, mink and blue herons.

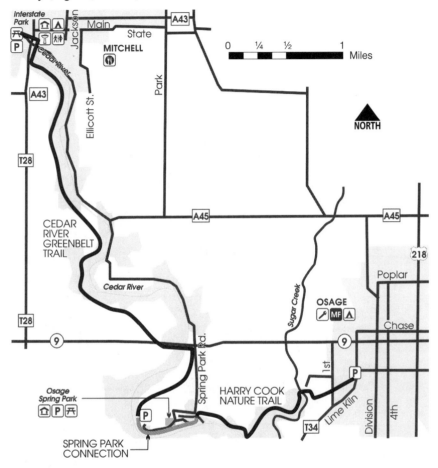

Charles City

Floyd County Historical Museum Original turn of the century drugstore, restored 1853 log cabin. For antique tractor buffs, collection of information pertaining to the founders of the gasoline tractor industry, the Hart-Parr Company. 1913 Hart-Parr tractor on display. Location 500 Gilbert Street.

Charles City Art Center 1904 Carnegie building houses art gallery, art library and classroom. Permanent collection plus other exhibits and programs. Location 301 N. Jackson Street.

Grafton

Grafton Heritage Depot Turn of the century depot with waiting room, depot agents office, freight room. Upstairs houses local memorabilia. National Register of Historic Places. Location Main Street.

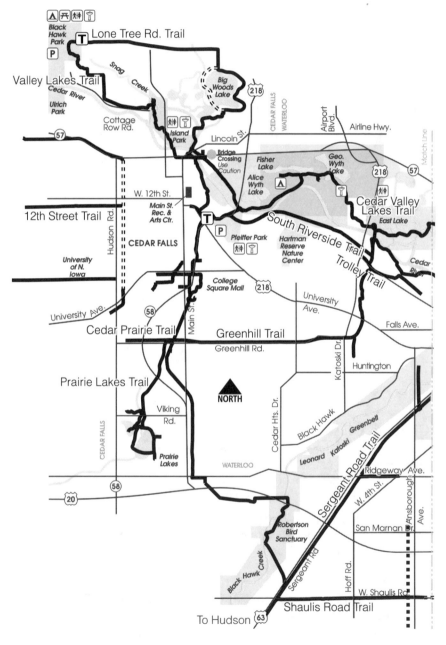

TRAIL LEGEND

————————	Bike/Multi Trail
••••••••••••	Hiking only Trail
✕✕✕✕✕✕✕✕✕	XC Skiing only
==========	Planned Trail
‑ ‑ ‑ ‑ ‑ ‑	Alternate Trail
————————	Road/Highway
+++++++++++	Railroad Tracks

Lone Tree Rd. Trail

Black Hawk Park

Valley Lakes Trail

Snag Creek

Big Woods Lake

218

Cedar River

Ulrich Park

Cottage Row Rd.

Island Park

CEDAR FALLS
WATERLOO

Airport Blvd.

Airline Hwy.

Match Line

Lincoln St.

Bridge Crossing Use Caution

Fisher Lake

Geo. Wyth Lake

218

57

57

Alice Wyth Lake

Cedar Valley Lakes Trail

East Lake

W. 12th St.

12th Street Trail

Main St. Rec. & Arts Ctr.

Hudson Rd.

CEDAR FALLS

Pfeiffer Park

Hartman Reserve Nature Center

South Riverside Trail

Trolley Trail

Cedar River

University of N. Iowa

College Square Mall

218

University Ave.

Falls Ave.

University Ave.

58

Cedar Prairie Trail

Main St.

Greenhill Trail

Greenhill Rd.

Katoski Dr.

Huntington

Prairie Lakes Trail

NORTH

Viking Rd.

Cedar Hts. Dr.

Black Hawk

Greenbelt

CEDAR FALLS

Prairie Lakes

WATERLOO

Leonard Katoski

Sergeant Road Trail

Ridgeway Ave.

58

W. 4th St.

Ansborough Ave.

20

Robertson Bird Sanctuary

San Marnan Dr.

Black Hawk Creek

Sergeant Rd.

Hoff Rd.

W. Shaulis Rd.

To Hudson

63

Shaulis Road Trail

George Wyth State Park Sergeant Road Trail

Trail Length	70.0 miles
Surface	Concrete, asphalt, limestone screenings, unimproved
Vicinity	Waterloo, Cedar Falls
Location & Setting	A recreational trail system uniting the park and recreation facilities of Waterloo and Cedar Falls. These two cities offer many cultural opportunities in addition to their excellent trails.
Information	Black Hawk County Conservation Board (319) 266-6813 Eastern Iowa Tourism Association (800) 891-3482

County   Black Hawk

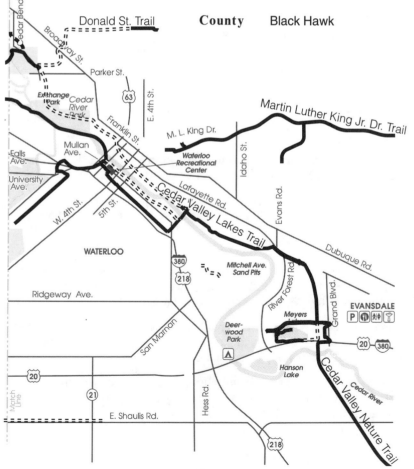

George Wyth State Park

In addition to the 5.5 miles of multi-use trails there are 6 miles of grass hiking trails. The park has a large expanse of woodland with many varieties of wildlife, with over 200 different species of birds observed and white-tailed deer year-round. Picnicking and camping facilities are available.

Waterloo Attractions

Rensselaer Russell House Museum Mid-Victorian house for three generations of Russells. One of the oldest homes in Black Hawk County. Location 520 W. Third St.

Waterloo Museum of Art Has a junior art gallery. Location 225 Commercial St.

Bluedorn Science Imaginarium Experiment with physics, light, sound and momentum. Daily demonstrations, laser show, interactive exhibits. Location 322 Washington.

Grout Museum of History and Science Daily planetarium shows, interactive "Discovery Zone". Learn about natural history & Native Americans. Location 503 South St.

Cedar Falls Attractions

James & Meryl Hearst Center for the Arts Two galleries featuring various exhibits throughout the year. Location 304 W. Seerley Blvd.

Victorian Home & Carriage House Museum Built in 1861 and re-stored to elegant 1890 Victorian life. Gowned mannequins in period clothing. Location 300 W. 3rd.

Little Red Schoolhouse 1909 one-room school with desks, blackboards, books, bell tower, pot-bellied stove, see a typical day in an old-fashioned school setting. Location First & Clay Streets.

Ice House Museum Items used in harvesting, storing, and selling natural ice as in the early 1900's. A 1920s kitchen, horse drawn school hack, buggies, sleighs, a 1909 REO. Location First & Clay Sts.

Hartman Reserve Nature Center 80 acre woodland in the heart of Black Hawk County. 5 miles of trails and three bridges, ideal for photography, hiking, x-c skiing & nature study. Location 657 Reserve Dr.

George Wyth House and Viking Pump Museum Family home refurbished in the Art Deco style. Research library on the Art Deco period of 1925 to 1935 Location 303 Franklin St.

George Wyth State Park

Trail Length	5.5 miles
Surface	Asphalt, concrete
Vicinity	Waterloo, Cedar Falls
Location & Setting	One of the trails making up the Cedar Valley Lakes Trail Network. Located on the Cedar River within the Waterloo-Cedar Falls metropolitan area.
Information	George Wyth State Park (319) 232-5505

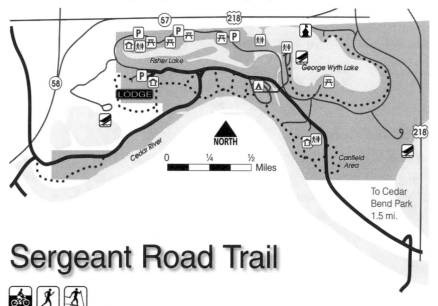

Sergeant Road Trail

Trail Length	10.0 miles
Surface	Crushed stone
Vicinity	Hudson, Waterloo
Location & Setting	The Sergeant Road Trail parallels Hwy 63 from Waterloo to Hudson through rural and park areas. It is built on abandoned rail grade. Parking is available at Waterloo and Westfield Avenue, a block north of Hwy 218, and at Shaulis Road and Hwy 63 south of Hwy 20.
Information	Cedar Falls Parks Division (319) 273-8625
County	Black Hawk

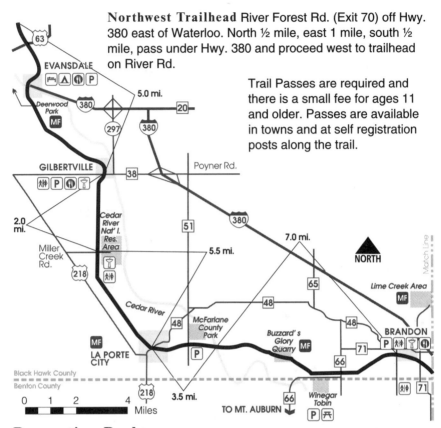

Northwest Trailhead River Forest Rd. (Exit 70) off Hwy. 380 east of Waterloo. North ½ mile, east 1 mile, south ½ mile, pass under Hwy. 380 and proceed west to trailhead on River Rd.

Trail Passes are required and there is a small fee for ages 11 and older. Passes are available in towns and at self registration posts along the trail.

Recreation Parks

Wakema Park	Picnicking, water, restroom, parking, playground
Wild Cat Bluff Area	Boating, fishing, picnicking, camping, water, restroom, parking
Line Creek Area	Picnicking, camping, fishing, water, restrooms, shelter, parking
Winegar Tobin	Boating, fishing, picnicking, parking
McFarlane County Park	Picnicking, hiking, camping, fishing, shelter, water, restrooms, showers, parking, playground (138 acres).
Cedar River Natural Resource Area	Restroom, river access (540 acres)

ROUTE SLIP	INTERVAL	TOTAL
Hiawatha (SE Trailhead)		
Hwy. 34 (Cnty. Home Rd.)	4.5	4.5
Lafayette (Midway)	4.5	9.0
Center Point (Lewis)	5.0	14.0
Urbana (Hwy. 26)	6.5	20.5
Brandon (Hwy. 48)	8.5	29.0
Cedar Rvr. (McFarlane Pk.)	7.0	36.0
LaPorte City (Hwy. 48)	3.5	39.5
Miller Creek Road	5.5	45.0
Gilbertville (Hwy. 38)	2.0	46.5
Evansdale (NW Trailhead)	5.0	52.0

Cedar Valley Nature Trail

Trail Length	52.0 miles
Surface	Crushed limestone, asphalt – 16 miles on the northern end between Branson and Waterloo, and 4 miles on the southern end between Hiawatha and County Home Road.
Vicinity	Evansdale, Brandon, Hiawatha
Location & Setting	The trail is built on an abandoned rail bed between Cedar Rapids and Waterloo, Iowa. It's a nationally designated recreation trail and is part of the American Discovery Trail. Historical landmarks, archaeological sites and restored railroad depots at Gilbertville and Center Point add interest to the trail. Facilities at Fross Park in Center Point include water, restrooms, picnicking, shelters, and parking. Wildlife in the area includes deer, woodchucks, wild turkey, badgers and songbirds.

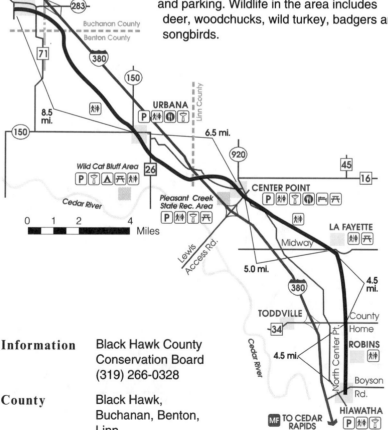

Information	Black Hawk County Conservation Board (319) 266-0328
County	Black Hawk, Buchanan, Benton, Linn

Chichaqua Valley Trail

Trail Length	20.0 miles
Surface	Asphalt
Vicinity	Bondurant, Baxter
Location & Setting	The trail crosses the forested banks and timbered bluffs of the Skunk River on an old railbed. The area offers a variety of scenic and diverse wildlife. Open spaces, farmland, wooded areas and small communities.
Information	Polk County Conservation Board (515) 323-5300 Jasper County Conservation Board (641) 792-9780
County	Polk. Jasper

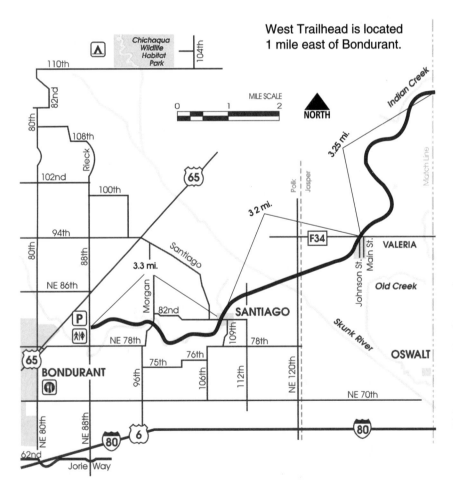

West Trailhead is located 1 mile east of Bondurant.

Baxter Trailhead

Exit Hwy. 223 onto Main St. for half a mile. The trail begins behind the State Savings Bank and is a short block from the center of town. There is parking, shelter and a picnic area is available.

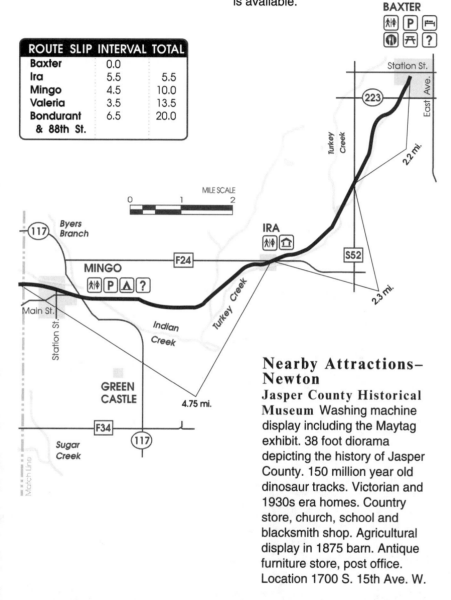

ROUTE SLIP	INTERVAL	TOTAL
Baxter	0.0	
Ira	5.5	5.5
Mingo	4.5	10.0
Valeria	3.5	13.5
Bondurant & 88th St.	6.5	20.0

Nearby Attractions– Newton

Jasper County Historical Museum Washing machine display including the Maytag exhibit. 38 foot diorama depicting the history of Jasper County. 150 million year old dinosaur tracks. Victorian and 1930s era homes. Country store, church, school and blacksmith shop. Agricultural display in 1875 barn. Antique furniture store, post office. Location 1700 S. 15th Ave. W.

Trail Rules

The trail is closed from 10:30 PM to 5:00 AM. Motorized vehicles and horses are not permitted on the trail. Snowmobiles are allowed on the Jasper County segment when snow cover is adequate.

Cinder Path

⊞ 🚴 𝑅 ⛷ ∩ 🛷

Trail Length	15.0 miles
Surface	Cinder, crushed limestone
Vicinity	Chariton, Humeston
Location & Setting	South central Iowa between Chariton in Lucas County and Humeston in Wayne County. Built on abandoned railroad right of way. The trail is lined with native Iowa timber, with prairie areas and abundant wildlife.
Information	Lucas County Conservation Board (515) 774-2433
County	Lucas, Wayne

Adjoining the Cinder Path north of Chariton's Business 34 is the 1.5 mile Lucas County Conservation Exercise Trail, with 13 stations, from warm-up activities to aerobic activities and ending with cool-down muscle relaxers.

The even grade and smooth cinder surface of the Cinder Path makes the trail ideal for bikers and hikers. The path includes 16 wooden bridges, a covered bridge and a 20 foot lookout tower.

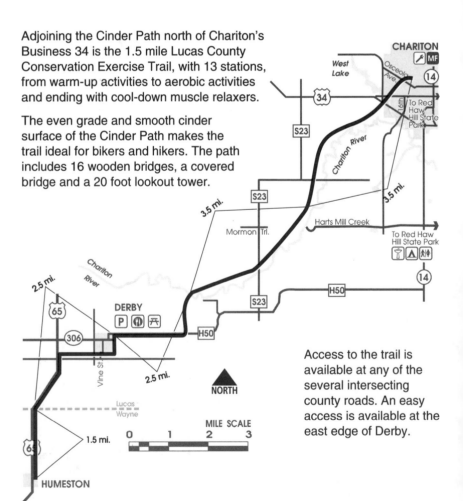

Access to the trail is available at any of the several intersecting county roads. An easy access is available at the east edge of Derby.

40

Clinton Discovery Trail
Riverview Park Recreational Trail

Trail Length	5.0 miles
Surface	Paved
Vicinity	Clinton
Location & Setting	Located in Clinton, along the Mississippi River, extending from Hwy 30 on the south to Eagle Point Park on the north. Restroom, water, & picnic facilities available at Eagle Point & Riverview Parks.
Information	Clinton Parks Department (563) 243-1260
County	Clinton

Clive Greenbelt Trail

Trail Length	8.50 miles
Surface	Asphalt
Vicinity	Clive
Location & Setting	The Clive Greenbelt Trail is some 8.5 miles of scenic, heavily wooded trail through a greenbelt in the city of Clive, just west of Des Moines. The trail links with the Campbell Recreation Area which has concessions, picnic areas, restrooms and parking. There is a large selection of lodging and restaurants near the trail.
Information	Clive Park & Recreation Dept. (515) 223-5246
County	Polk

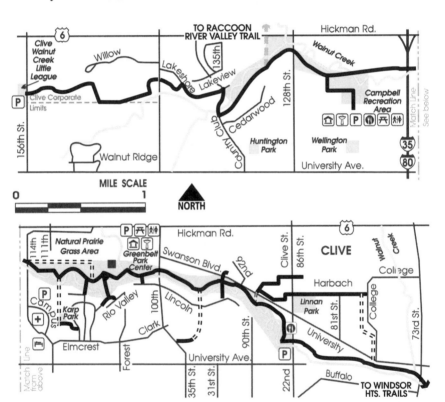

Trailheads (Accesses with Parking)

1400 block of 86th St. (east trailhead) • 1500 block of 100th St. • 114th Street • NW 156th St. (west trailhead) • Campbell Recreation Area

Comet Trail

Trail Length	7.0 miles
Surface	Crushed limestone (8' wide)
Vicinity	Conrad
Location & Setting	From Conrad, through Beaman & east with a spur into Wolf Creek Recreation Area in Grundy County and a half mile into Tama County in Northeast Iowa. Built on a segment of the old Chicago and Northwestern line. Open areas, farmland, prairie, small communities.
Information	Grundy County Conservation Board (319) 345-2688
County	Grundy, Tama

Bicycle sales and service are available in Grundy Center, Hwy 14-175, 12 miles northwest of Beaman.

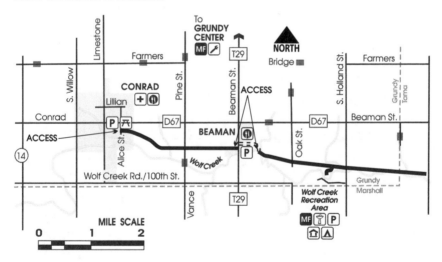

Accesses

Conrad South end of Alice Street

Beaman West side of County Road T-29. East side - ½ mile east of County Road T-29 and south

Wolf Creek RA Northeast corner of Wolf Creek Recreation Area (2 miles east and ½ mile south from Beaman)

Riverfront Trail
Duck Creek Parkway Trail

Trail Length	Duck Creek Parkway Trail	13.5 miles
	Riverfront Trail	6.0 miles

Surface   Asphalt and concrete

Vicinity   Davenport, Bettendorf

Location & Setting   Davenport/Bettendorf. Located in an urban greenbelt, combining woodlands, wetlands and urban housing surroundings. The terrain is flat and gently rolling.

Information   Davenport Parks & Recreation   (563) 344-4113

County   Scott

Festivals and outdoor activities in the Quad Cities extend from spring through winter.

Davenport Attractions

The Putnam Museum of History & Natural Science Mississippi River Valley wildlife, Asian & Egyptian galleries, 3500 year old mummy. Location 1717 W. 12th St.

International Fire Museum 1951 Mack pumper truck, hand drawn hose carts, uniforms, etc., all housed in a 1931 firehouse. Location 2301 E. 11th St.

Mississippi River Visitor Center Learn about the lock & dam system on the Mississippi and watch boats passing through Lock & Dam #15. Location Western tip of Arsenal Island.

Colonel Davenport Historic Home 1833 army fort construction that brought George Davenport here in 1816. Location Arsenal Island on the Mississippi River.

Davenport Museum of Art Closed Mondays & holidays. Location 1737 W. 12th St.

Mississippi Valley Welcome Center On a scenic overlook, great view of the Mississippi River. Looks like an old riverboat captain's home. Brochures & information. Location: 900 Eagle Ridge Rd., Le Claire.

Buffalo Bill Cody Homestead Home of the Cody family built in 1847. Restored home, stagecoach. Location 28050 230th Ave., Princeton.

Buffalo Bill Museum "Buffalo Bill" Memorial as well as a steamboat museum. Location 200 N. River Dr., Le Claire.

The Duck Creek Parkway Trail follows the Duck Creek tributary from Emeis Park through Duck Creek Park to Central Avenue and Devil's Glen Park in Bettendorf.

The Riverfront Trail follows the Mississippi River from Mound Street to Credit Island Park. There is a new bicycle/pedestrian bridge over the Mississippi called the American Discovery Bridge.

Decorah City Trails

Ice Cave Hill

Trail Length | 1.25 miles

Surface/ Setting | Ungroomed, moderate to difficult trails winding through pine and other native trees.

Lower Ice Cave

Trail Length | 1.0 mile

Surface/ Setting | Natural, flat trail winding along the Upper Iowa River.

Van Peenen Park

Trail Length | 4.0 miles

Surface/ Setting | Double-track, easy to moderate trails through native prairie and pine trees.

Palisades Park

Trail Length | 2.0 miles

Surface/ Setting | Double-track, moderate to difficult. Trails show a spectacular view of Decorah. Picnic facilities are available.

Oneota Drive Recreational Trail

Trail Length | 2.5 mile

Surface/ Setting | 1.0 mile groomed double-track, easy to moderate. 1.5 mile asphalt - 8' wide. Trail winds along the Upper Iowa River and scenic Phelps Park bluffs.

Twin Springs

Trail Length | 0.75 miles

Surface/ Setting | Ungroomed trail overlooking Twin Springs trout stream. Moderate to difficult.

Information | Decorah Parks and Recreation   (563) 382-4158

County | Winneshiek

🚴 Leisure Biking
🚵 Mountain Biking
🚶 Hiking
⛷ Cross-country Skiing
🐎 Horseback Riding
🛼 Rollerblading
🛷 Other

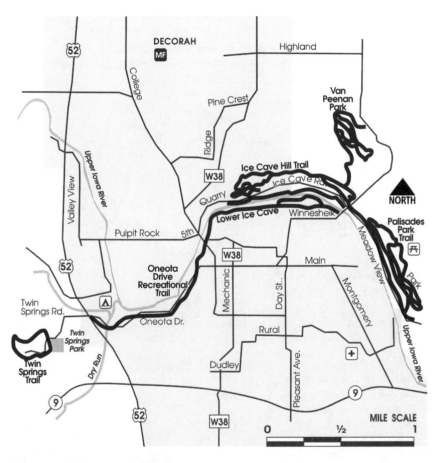

Decorah Attractions

Vesterheim the Norwegian-American Museum America's oldest and largest museum devoted to one immigrant ethnic group. Vesterheim features objects from life in old Norway to the Atlantic Crossing to establishing life in pioneer America. Highlights are actual homes and buildings from Norway & pioneer immigrant America, the North Dakota prairie, a 25' ship that sailed across the Atlantic, colorful costumes, hand-crafted decorative fold arts, fine arts by immigrant artists, a comprehensive display of pioneer immigrant farming equipment. Location 502 W. Water St.

Dubuque Area
Floodwall Trail

Trail Length	3.0 miles	North section	2.2 miles
		South section	0.8 miles

Surface   Paved

Vicinity   Dubuque

Location
& Setting   Along the Mississippi riverfront in Dubuque. North Section: North to look at the dam. South Section: Jones Street east to parking by floodwall. Proceed south.

Information   Dubuque Visitors Bureau   **(563) 657-9200**

County   Dubuque

Area Attractions

Dubuque Iowa Welcome Center Travel information along with rest facilities in Dubuque's historic Ice Harbor. Location Third St.

Cable Car Square Cable Car elevator, charming shops, boutiques, and eateries. Location: 4th Street and Bluff St.

Fenelon Place Elevator Company The world's shortest, steepest scenic railway. From 4th St. to Fenelon Place. Magnificent view of three states and the Mississippi River. Location 512 Fenelon Pl.

Crystal Lake Cave ¾ mile of well lit passageways with intricate formations and underground lake. The rare formations are known as anthrodites and the cave is a constant 50 degrees F.

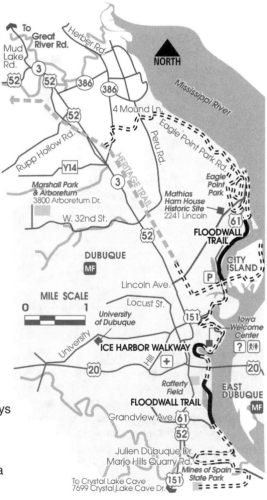

East River Trail

Trail Length	5.5 miles
Surface	Asphalt
Vicinity	Des Moines
Location & Setting	Located in the city of Des Moines. The north trailhead is at McHenry Park (8th & Oak Park Ave.). The south trailhead is at Hawthorn Park (SE 14th & Railroad Ave.) Convenient accesses with parking at Birdland Park (Birdland Drive & Saylor Road) and at Crivaro Park (E. 1st and Grand Ave.).
Information	Des Moines Parks & Recreation (515) 237-1386 Des Moines Visitors Bureau (515) 286-4950
County	Polk

The trail follows the Des Moines River through the city, passing the Sec Taylor Baseball Stadium and the old Riverview Park. The north end of the trail connects to the Saylorville-Des Moines River Trail.

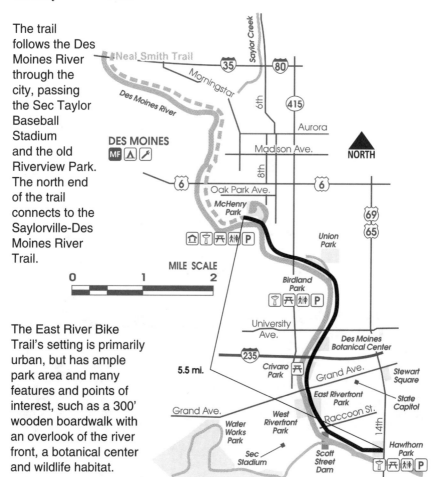

The East River Bike Trail's setting is primarily urban, but has ample park area and many features and points of interest, such as a 300' wooden boardwalk with an overlook of the river front, a botanical center and wildlife habitat.

Fairfield Loop Trail

Trail Length	13.0 miles, plus 6 miles planned
Surface	Crushed limestone
Vicinity	Fairfield
Location & Setting	The Fairfield Loop Trail encircles the town of Fairfield in southeast Iowa. When complete it will total approximately 19 miles and will connect to another 12 miles of trails in other parks.
Information	Jefferson County Conservation Board (641) 472-4421
County	Jefferson

Trail Sections

1 North Section	4.1 miles
2 BNSF Trail	1.0 miles
3 Lamson Woods	0.5 miles
4 Erma Hartman Trail	0.5 miles
Jefferson County Park	7.0 miles
5 Cedar View Trail	1.5 miles

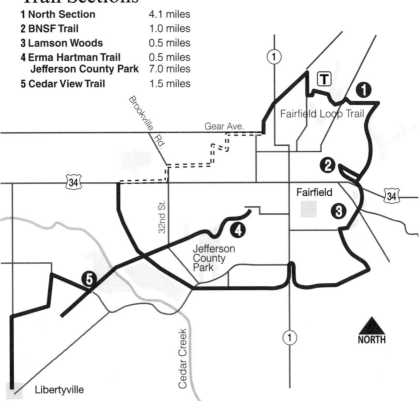

Fort Dodge Nature Trail

Trail Length	3.7 miles
Surface	Crushed limestone
Vicinity	Fort Dodge
Location & Setting	The nature trail is located between William's Drive and County Road D14 and built on abandoned railbed.
Information	Fort Dodge Parks Department (515) 576-7237
County	Webster

One point of interest is the Fort Dodge Museum, which includes a pioneer village with collections of pioneer, military and Native American exhibits, and a replica of the Cardiff Giant, a famous hoax carved from a piece of Ford Dodge Gypsum.

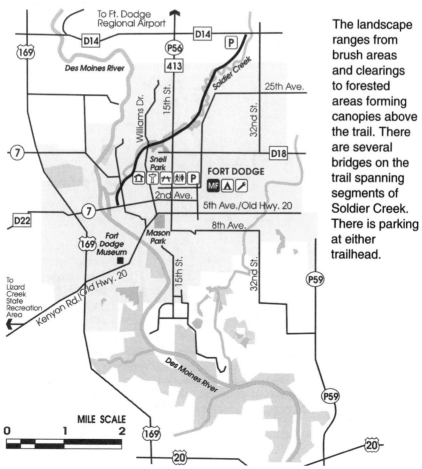

The landscape ranges from brush areas and clearings to forested areas forming canopies above the trail. There are several bridges on the trail spanning segments of Soldier Creek. There is parking at either trailhead.

Four Mile Creek Greenway Trail
Gay Lea Wilson Trail

Trail Length	11.0 miles (35 miles when completed)
Surface	Asphalt, 12 feet wide
Vicinity	Altoona, Pleasant Hill
Location & Setting	This trail system, with 8 miles currently completed, will stretch from the Saylorville Lake are to Yellow Banks county Park on the Des Moines River and the Chichaqua Valley Trail. It will be a vital link in the central Iowa "100 mile loop". The surface is asphalt, and 12-feet wide. The setting varies from urban to open and wooded, running through a combination of railroad and greenway corridors.
Information	Polk County Conservation Board (515) 323-5300 Des Moines Parks & Recreation (515) 263-8709
County	Polk

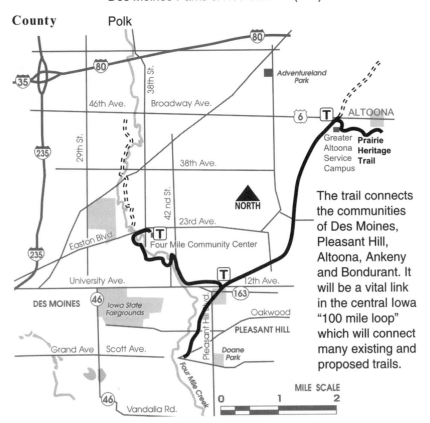

The trail connects the communities of Des Moines, Pleasant Hill, Altoona, Ankeny and Bondurant. It will be a vital link in the central Iowa "100 mile loop" which will connect many existing and proposed trails.

Franklin Grove
Heritage Trail

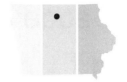

Trail Length	1.8 miles
Surface	Asphalt
Vicinity	Belmond
Location & Setting	The trail is built on an abandoned railbed and runs north and south through the residential section of Belmond and into rural areas. There are accesses at street intersections.
Information	Belmond Chamber of Commerce (641) 444-3937
County	Wright

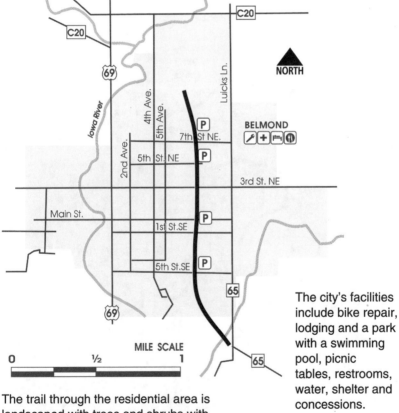

The city's facilities include bike repair, lodging and a park with a swimming pool, picnic tables, restrooms, water, shelter and concessions.

The trail through the residential area is landscaped with trees and shrubs with convenient benches. The north end of the trail is primarily native grasses while the south end is largely woodland and brush.

Geode State Park

Trail Length	6.0 miles
Surface	Natural
Vicinity	Burlington
Location & Setting	Located in the southeast corner of Iowa, this 6-mile trail loops around Geode Lake. It's single-track, and the effort level ranges from easy to moderate with a few short, steep hills. The setting is rolling, hardwood forest. The Park entrance can be accessed off Rte 79, 10-miles west of Burlington.
Information	Geode State Park (319) 392-4601
County	Des Moines

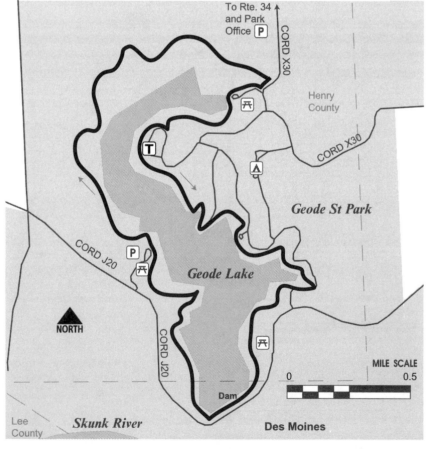

Great Western Trail

Trail Length	18.0 miles
Surface	Asphalt
Vicinity	Des Moines, Martensdale
Location & Setting	A 18 mile trail running from Des Moines to Martensdale, and built on abandoned rail bed. The trail is relatively flat, with rich meadows, prairie grasses, streams, and wooded areas.

Information
Polk County
Conservation Board
(515) 323-5300

Warren County
Conservation Board
(515) 961-6169

County
Polk, Warren

North trailhead
Across from the
Izaak Walton League
Clubhouse on Valley
Drive in Des Moines.

Restaurants and
restroom are
available near
the Des Moines
and Martensdale
trailheads, in
Cumming and
Orilla. Picnic area,
shelters and water
are located at
Gear Street north
of Martensdale,
Coolidge Street
south of Cumming
and south of 72nd
Avenue in Polk
County.

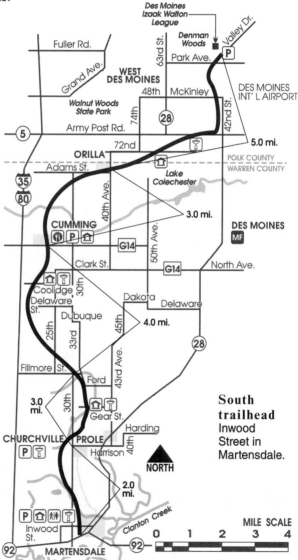

Des Moines Izaak Walton League
Denman Woods
Valley Dr.
Fuller Rd.
63rd St.
Park Ave.
P
WEST DES MOINES
48th McKinley
DES MOINES INT'L AIRPORT
Walnut Woods State Park
74th
28
42nd St.
Grand Ave.
Army Post Rd.
5
72nd
5.0 mi.
ORILLA
Adams St.
POLK COUNTY
WARREN COUNTY
35
80
40th Ave.
Lake Colechester
3.0 mi.
CUMMING
G14
50th Ave.
DES MOINES
MF
Clark St.
G14
North Ave.
Coolidge
30th
Delaware St.
Dakota
Delaware
25th
Dubuque
45th
4.0 mi.
33rd
28
Fillmore St.
Ford
43rd Ave.
3.0 mi.
30th
Gear St.
Harding
CHURCHVILLE PROLE
Harrison
40th
NORTH
South trailhead
Inwood
Street in
Martensdale.
2.0 mi.
P
Inwood St.
Clanton Creek
MILE SCALE
0 1 2 3 4
92
MARTENSDALE
92

Heart of Iowa Nature Trail

Trail Length	32 miles (17 completed)
Surface	Crushed limestone
Vicinity	Melbourne, Slater
Location & Setting	From Melbourne, west to Slater in Iowa's heartland. Built on an abandoned Milwaukee Railbed. There are significant prairie remnants east of Slater, heavily wooded tracts near Cambridge and Maxwell and wetland areas west of Cambridge. Surface is crushed limestone, with segments incomplete between Collins and Rhodes. This trail is a link in the American Discovery Trail.
Information	Marshall County Conservation Board (641) 752-5490
County	Story, Marshall

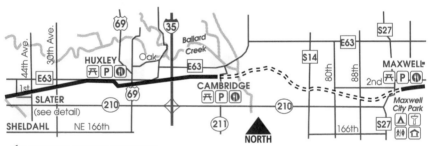

◢ **To Saylorville-Des Moines River Trail**

MILE SCALE
0 1 2 3 4

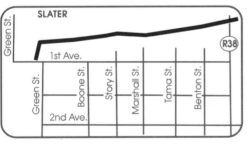

Slater Access
Trailhead is on R33 (Lynn St.) just north of town. There is parking. water. a picnic area and shelter available.

There is a small trail user's fee.

Future plans for the Heart of Iowa Nature Trail include connecting the west trail portion to the Saylorville-Des Moines Trail and the east trail portion to the Chichaqua Valley Trail, making a 100 mile loop.

TRAIL LEGEND

———	Bike/Multi Trail
••••••••••	Hiking only Trail
▪▪▪▪▪▪▪▪▪	XC Skiing only
==========	Planned Trail
▩ ▩ ▩ ▩ ▩	Alternate Trail
———	Road/Highway
┼┼┼┼┼┼┼┼┼	Railroad Tracks

Route Slip	Interval	Total
Melbourne		
Rhodes	4.8	4.8
Hoy Bridge	1.7	6.5
Collins	5.1	11.6
Maxwell	5.0	16.6
Cambridge	7.0	23.6
Huxley	3.5	27.1
Slater	4.5	31.6

The Hoy Bridge, a concrete arch bridge built in 1912, is 60 feet high and 212 feet long. This bridge is only accessible from the trail and is a major attraction on the Heart of Iowa Trail with its view of Clear Creek Valley lying beyond.

Melbourne Access Trailhead is at the corner of 290th and Hart but is undeveloped.

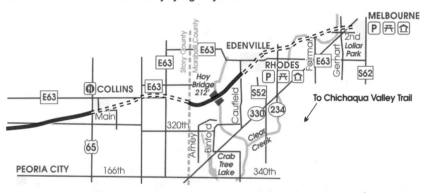

Heritage Trail

Trail Length	26.0 miles
Surface	Crushed limestone
Vicinity	Dubuque, Dyersville
Location & Setting	Located in northeastern Iowa and built on a segment of the Old Chicago Great Western railbed. It runs westerly from just north of Dubuque to Dyersville. The trail provides rugged woodlands, river overlooks, limestone bluffs and primitive prairies. Trail Grade = 1% maximum.
Information	Swiss Valley Nature Center (319) 556-6745 Dubuque County Conservation Board (563) 556-6745
County	Dubuque

Dyersville Attractions

The Ertl Company Tour the plant of authentic toy replicas of tractors, planes, cars, trucks, etc. & toy store. Location Hwys. 136 & 20.

Basilica of St. Francis Xavier One of 33 basilicas in U.S. True medieval Gothic architecture. Designated a Basilica in 1956. Twin spires are 212 feet tall. Location Corner of 2nd St. SW & 1st Ave.

National Farm Toy Museum Farm toys, trucks and other toys of interest. Displays illustrate the history and importance of agriculture. Location 1110 - 16th Ave. SE Located at Hwy 136 & 20.

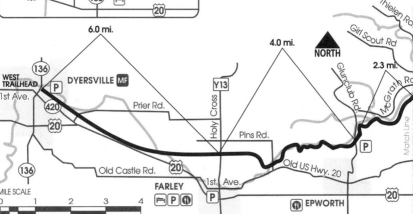

Along the trail are opportunities to visit interpretive sites, railroad artifacts, fossil collections, old lead mines and interesting communities. There is a small trail fee.

For more information contact:
Tourist Information Center
(319) 556-4372

Route Slip	Interval	Total
Dubuque	0.0	0.0
East Trailhead	3.0	3.0
Durango	4.0	7.0
Graf	8.0	15.0
Epworth	4.0	19.0
Farley	4.0	23.0
Dyersville	6.0	29.0

Dubuque Attractions

Mathias Ham House Historic Site 1833 Double log house with hands-on exhibit. 1856 Italian limestone mansion authentically restored and furnished. Location: 2241 Lincoln Ave.

Dubuque Museum of Art National Historic Landmark offers a variety of exhibitions annually. The Wm. & Adelaide Glab Children's Gallery presents interactive, hands-on exhibitions. Location: 36 E. 8th St.

Dubuque Arboretum/Botanical Gardens Award-winning garden displays flowers & vegetables, prairie grasses & wildflowers, water gardens, waterfalls & ornamental plantings. Location: 3800 Arboretum Dr.

Mississippi River Museum Life-sized exhibits covering 300 years of river history. See the Sidewheeler William M. Black, a 277 ft. dredge boat now a National Landmark. Location: 3rd Street Ice Harbor.

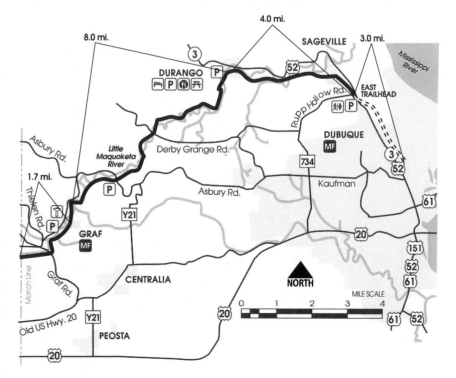

Hoover Nature Trail

Trail Length	32.0 miles (17 miles complete)
Surface	Crushed limestone
Vicinity	Burlington, Cedar Rapids
Location & Setting	Located in southeast Iowa and built along abandoned railroad right-a-way. When completed it will extend from Cedar Rapids to Muscatine, and will be a link in the American Discovery Trail. Setting is prairie, farmland, and some heavily timbered areas. Horseback riding is restricted to marked paths.
Information	Story County Conservation Board (515) 232-2515
County	Blackhawk, Benton, Linn, Johnson, Muscatine, Louisa

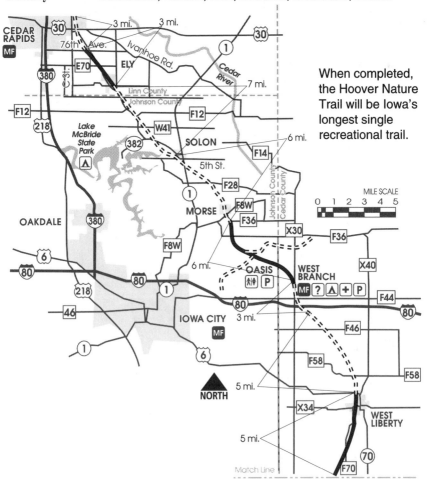

When completed, the Hoover Nature Trail will be Iowa's longest single recreational trail.

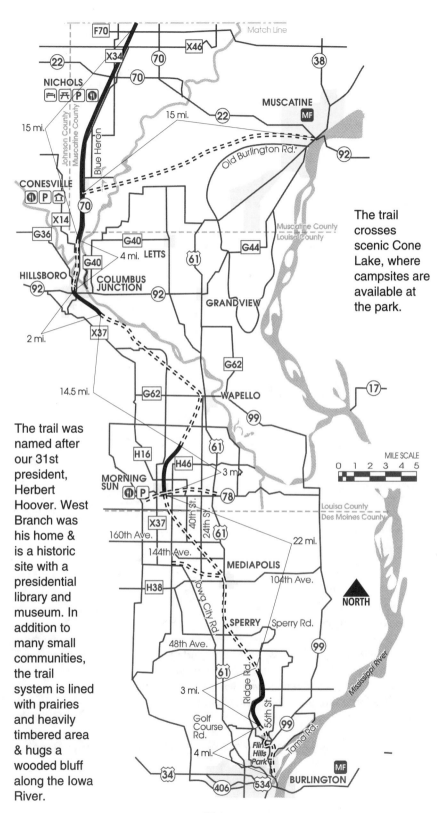

The trail crosses scenic Cone Lake, where campsites are available at the park.

The trail was named after our 31st president, Herbert Hoover. West Branch was his home & is a historic site with a presidential library and museum. In addition to many small communities, the trail system is lined with prairies and heavily timbered area & hugs a wooded bluff along the Iowa River.

Location & Setting

The Iowa River Corridor Trail parallels the Iowa River and provides access to the center of Iowa City and the University of Iowa. It travels between Napoleon Park in south Iowa City and the Coralville Reservoir north of Iowa City and east of Coralville. There is parking for access at Napoleon Park, City Park, Ned Ashton Park, Crandic Park, and Waterworks Prairie Park.

The Coralville Clear Creek, North Ridge and North Liberty Trails combine to provide an 8 mile long trail serving the western portion of this metro area. It provides access to the Coral Ridge Mall, North Ridge Park, the Oakdale Campus, and the North Liberty Community Center. The trail route includes a pedestrian tunnel underneath I-80.

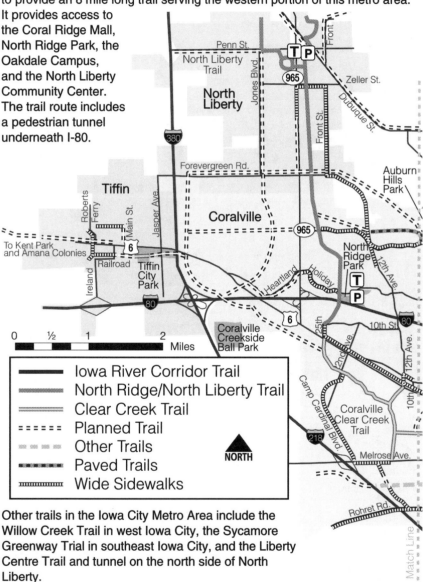

Iowa River Corridor Trail
North Ridge/North Liberty Trail
Clear Creek Trail
Planned Trail
Other Trails
Paved Trails
Wide Sidewalks

NORTH

Other trails in the Iowa City Metro Area include the Willow Creek Trail in west Iowa City, the Sycamore Greenway Trial in southeast Iowa City, and the Liberty Centre Trail and tunnel on the north side of North Liberty.

Information	Johnson County Conservation Board	(319) 645-2315
County	Johnson	

Iowa City Metro Trails
Iowa River Corridor Trail (IRC)
North Ridge Trail/Clear Creek Trail

Trail Length	Iowa River Corridor 9.0 miles (14 miles when complete)
	North Ridge/Clear Creek 8.0 miles
Surface	Asphalt & concrete
Vicinity	Iowa City, Coralville, North Liberty

Iowa Great Lakes Trail

🚵 🚶 ⛷ 🛼 🏂

Trail Length	20.0 miles
Surface	Asphalt
Vicinity	Milford, Spirit Lake
Location & Setting	Northwest Iowa. The south trailhead is in Milford and extends from 23rd and Keokuk Street to Spirit Lake, primarily on abandoned rail corridor.
Information	Dickinson County Conservation Board (712) 338-4786
County	Dickinson

In addition to the trail, this map includes some sixty miles of signed routes on low traffic country roads. The Terril Loop is 31 miles long and designated by signs with a red dot. There are trailheads at the DNR boat ramp in Arnold and at the southern end of the Spine Trail in Milford. The Superior/Swan Lake Loop is 29 miles long and designated by signs with a blue dot. It has trailheads in Superior or at Minnewaukon State Park on the Iowa/Minnesota border.

Wetlands

Fen, Dickinson County

Fens are Iowa's most unique wetland type. They are found primarily along the margins of the freshly glaciated landscapes in north-central Iowa and scattered throughout northeastern Iowa. These wetlands are sustained by groundwater flow and include saturated peat deposits, often in mounded positions along hill slopes and stream terraces. The water is highly mineralized compared to most wetlands, and, as a result, fens contain numerous state-listed rare and endangered species. Because of their unique hydrology, fens are unlikely candidates for restoration

projects, and the few that still remain need to be protected. With each passing year, more people are realizing the value associated with the preservation of natural wetland systems. These sites are recognized not only for their recreational and wildlife benefits, but increasingly for their importance as part of the natural hydrologic cycle. The management and restoration of Iowa's wetlands needs to be a cooperative venture among all segments of the state's scientific community.

Photo by Carol Thompson
Courtesy of Iowa Department of Natural Resources

The setting includes wildlife areas, popular blue lakes, sandy beaches, specialty shops and the festive communities of Milford, Arnolds Park, Okoboji and Spirit Lake.

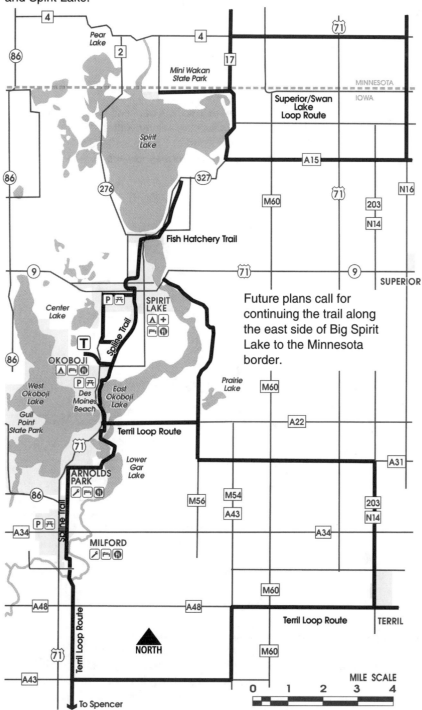

Jackson County Trail

Trail Length	3.8 miles
Surface	Crushed limestone
Vicinity	Spragueville
Location & Setting	Built on abandoned railbed, the Jackson County Recreation Trail parallels the Maquoketa River with trailheads at Z34 and 45th streets just north of Spragueville. Spragueville is approximately 40 miles southeast of Dubuque via Hwy. 61 south and Hwy. 64 east.
Information	Jackson County Conservation Board (563) 652-3783
County	Jackson

Emergency Assistance
Jackson County Sheriff
(563) 652-3312

Z20

Z20

P

Z34

Rockaway

MILE SCALE
0   1

VAN BUREN

Maquoketa River

Z20

45th St.

Main St.

P

SPRAGUEVILLE

▲ NORTH

Z34

113

64

PRESTON

Views of scenic bluffs and overlooks along the trail provide striking views of the Iowa river valley. The area has numerous local parks, wildlife areas and preserve. Maquoketa Caves State Park has rugged hiking trails providing spectacular views of geological formations and caves to explore. Bellevue State Park's hiking trails include Indian burial mounds, a historic mill, a quarry and a butterfly garden. Spruce Creek Park features boating and camping.

Jefferson County Park

Trail Length	7.0 miles
Surface	Limestone screenings
Vicinity	Fairfield
Location & Setting	Jefferson County Park is located just southwest of the town of Fairfield. The park entrance can be accessed off County Road H43 (south of Hwy. 34) or CR H33 (west of Hwy. 1).
Information	Jefferson County Conservation Board (515) 472-4421
County	Jefferson

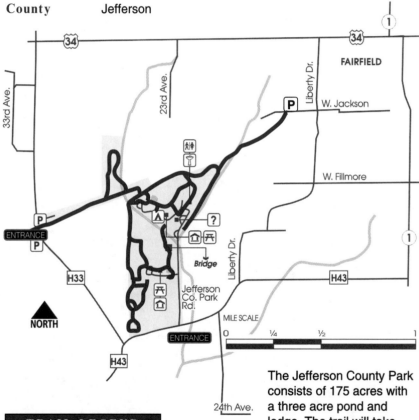

TRAIL LEGEND

————	Bike/Multi Trail
••••••••••	Hiking only Trail
▪▪▪▪▪▪▪▪	XC Skiing only
==========	Planned Trail
▬ ▬ ▬ ▬	Alternate Trail
————	Road/Highway
++++++++	Railroad Tracks

The Jefferson County Park consists of 175 acres with a three acre pond and lodge. The trail will take you through a diversity of landscapes including timber, prairies and meadows. A 75 foot swinging bridge is featured on the trail connecting the picnic area with the camp area.

Jordan Creek Trail

Trail Length	15.5 miles
Surface	Asphalt, concrete with crushed limestone (in Raccoon River Park)
Vicinity	West Des Moines
Location & Setting	Named for the creek that runs adjacent to the trail. It traverses wooded and open areas. Trailhead at 50th and E.P. True Parkway, at 22nd & Locust, & at south 39th and G.M. Mills Civic Pkwy.
Information	West Des Moines Parks & Recreation (515) 222-3444
County	Polk

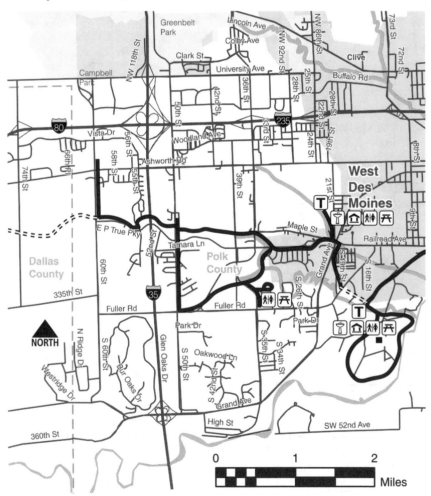

Kewash Nature Trail

Trail Length	13.8 miles
Surface	Crushed limestone
Vicinity	Washington, Keota
Location & Setting	Southeast Iowa, on a former railroad right-of-way running between the communities of Washington and Keota. The Kewash Nature Trail traverses a variety of landscape, from rich woodland area between Washington and West Chester to native prairie from West Chester to Keota.
Information	Washington County Conservation Board (319) 657-2400
County	Washington

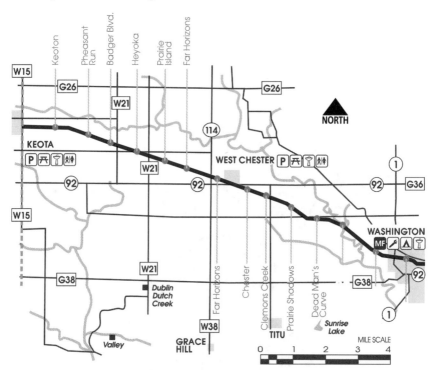

The trail provides the nature observer areas of rare and unusual plants such as silver sage, rattlesnake master, gentian, and blazing star. West of Washington, at Hays Timber, giant red oaks dominate the forest with their widespread branches.

There is a small trail fee for persons 16 years and older. Daily collection boxes are located at major road intersections.

Lake Ahquabi State Park

Trail Length	7.0 miles
Surface	Packed dirt, mowed grass, gravel
Vicinity	Indianola
Location & Setting	This trail is both single and double track. The setting is heavily wooded and hilly. Facilities included camping and a beach. From Indianola, 5-miles south on Hwy 65, then west a mile on Hwy 349 to the Park road.
Information	Lake Ahquabi State Park (515) 961-7101
County	Warren

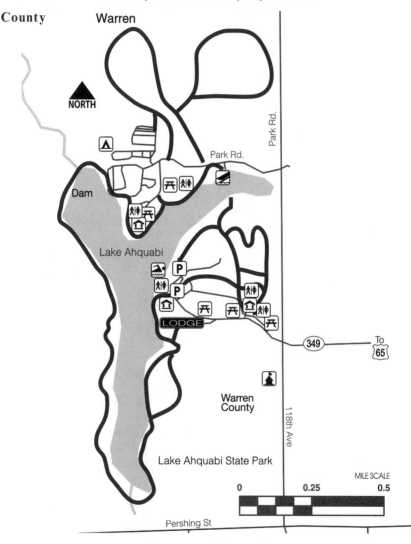

Lake Anita State Park

Trail Length	5.0 miles
Surface	Crushed limestone, paved
Vicinity	Atlantic, Anita
Location & Setting	The 1,062-acre Lake Anita State Park is one of the most popular outdoor recreation areas in southwest Iowa. The 171-acre artificial lake was formed by creating a dam on a branch of the Nishnabotna River. The 4 mile limestone surfaced trail runs completely around the lake, and connects to the mile long 10-foot wide paved Grass Roots Recreational Trail that runs from the Hwy 148 bridge to Anita. Facilities include picnic areas, shelters, a campground, restrooms, a swimming beach and boating.
Information	Lake Anita State Park (712) 762-4352
County	Cass

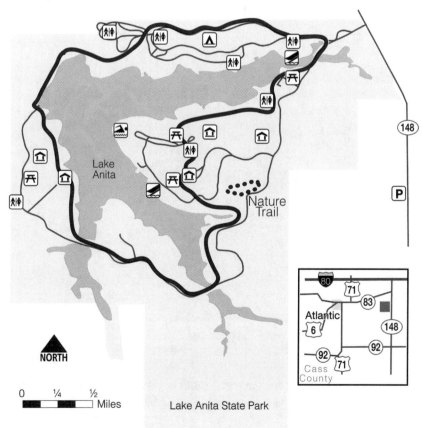

NORTH

0   ¼   ½ Miles

Lake Anita State Park

Lake MacBride State Park

Trail Length	5 miles, plus several miles of trails limited to cross-country skiing and hiking.
Surface	Gravel
Vicinity	Iowa City
Location & Setting	East central Iowa just west of Solon and between Cedar Rapids and Iowa City.
Information	Lake MacBridge State Park (319) 644-2200
County	Johnson

During the spring and fall, shorebirds, waterfowl and ospreys are frequent visitors.

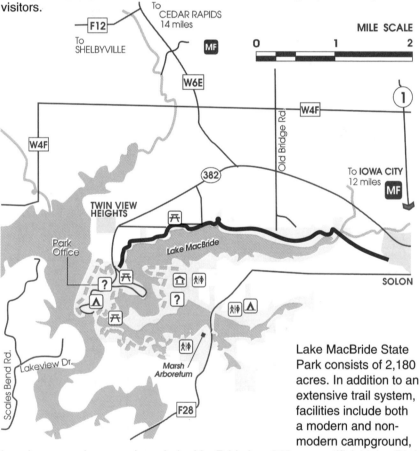

Lake MacBride State Park consists of 2,180 acres. In addition to an extensive trail system, facilities include both a modern and non-modern campground, beach area and concessions. Lake MacBride is a 812 acre artificial lake. Bird watchers will have the opportunity to sight nearly every songbird native to the region.

Lake Pahoja Recreation Trail

Trail Length	3.7 miles Bicycling is currently limited to 1.4 miles on the north side of the lake.
Surface	Asphalt for 1.4 miles, the remainder is grass
Vicinity	Larchwood
Location & Setting	Northwest corner of Iowa, 20 miles from Sioux Falls, South Dakota and 5 miles south of Larchwood. Exit Hwy. 182 to Hwy. A26 to access road.
Information	Lyon County Conservation Board (712) 472-2217
County	Lyon

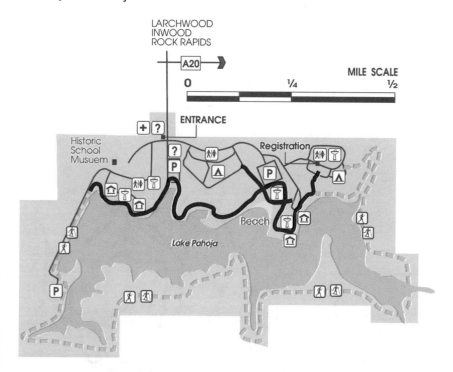

Lake Pahoja Recreation Area is a 232 acre highly developed, multi-use recreation area. Facilities include two lodges, playgrounds, campgrounds, beach and boat ramp. The lake is 69 acres.

Lime Creek Nature Center Trails

Trail Length	8.0 miles
Surface	Natural, groomed
Vicinity	Mason City
Location & Setting	Located two miles north of Mason City in north central Iowa. There is access by bicycle by way of the Winnebago Trail out of Mason City, or off Hwy 65 by auto. The trails wind through wetlands, woodlands, and prairies, providing an excellent way to view native plants and wildlife in their natural settings. The education facility includes live and mounted animals, and various natural resource displays. The park is closed for use from 10:30 pm to 6:00 am. Facilities include picnic areas and primitive camping.
Information	Cerro Gordo County Conservation Office (641) 423-5309
County	Cerro Gordo

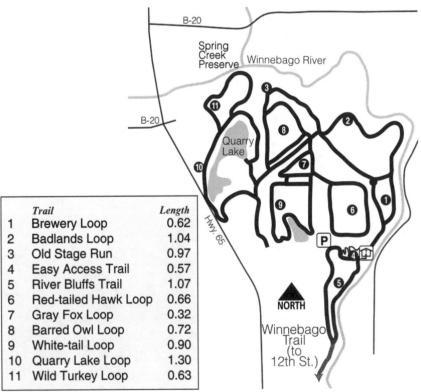

	Trail	Length
1	Brewery Loop	0.62
2	Badlands Loop	1.04
3	Old Stage Run	0.97
4	Easy Access Trail	0.57
5	River Bluffs Trail	1.07
6	Red-tailed Hawk Loop	0.66
7	Gray Fox Loop	0.32
8	Barred Owl Loop	0.72
9	White-tail Loop	0.90
10	Quarry Lake Loop	1.30
11	Wild Turkey Loop	0.63

Linn Creek Greenbelt

Trail Length	10.0 miles
Surface	Asphalt
Vicinity	Marshalltown
Location & Setting	Marshalltown in central Iowa. It is built on the dike that runs along Linn Creek and the Iowa River, and links several Marshalltown parks and recreation areas.
Information	Marshalltown Parks & Recreation (641) 754-5715
County	Marshall

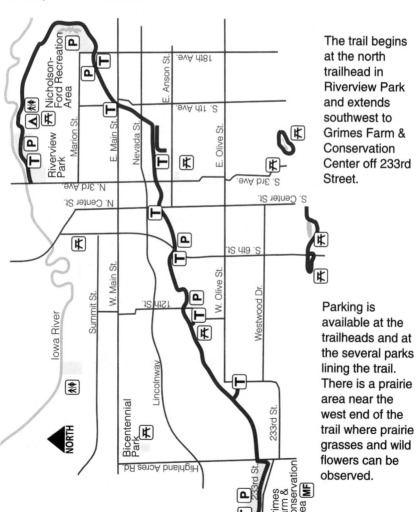

The trail begins at the north trailhead in Riverview Park and extends southwest to Grimes Farm & Conservation Center off 233rd Street.

Parking is available at the trailheads and at the several parks lining the trail. There is a prairie area near the west end of the trail where prairie grasses and wild flowers can be observed.

Matsell Bridge Natural Area

Trail Length	12.5 miles
Surface	Natural, groomed
Vicinity	Springville, Anamosa
Location & Setting	The Matsell Bridge Natural Area trails, located between Springville & Anamosa in East Central Iowa, consists of the 6.3-miles Pine & Prairie Trail and the 2.2-mile Red Oak Trail. The trails are looped, but don't intersect. The setting is both wooded and open area, with wetland in the northwest corner.
Information	Linn County 319-892-6450
County	Linn

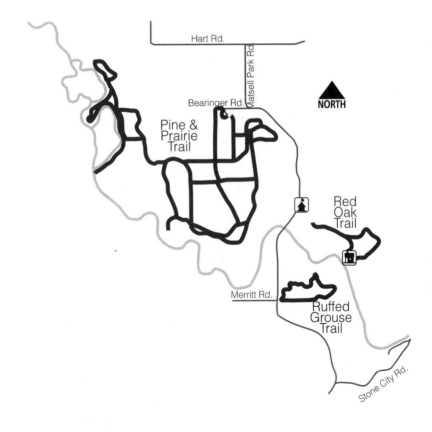

McFarland & Peterson County Parks

Trail Length	9.7 miles
Surface	Packed dirt and mowed grass
Vicinity	Ames
Location & Setting	The trails are mostly single track. The setting is forest, river bottoms and prairie. From Ames, north on CR R63 (Dayton Ave) for about 4-miles to the park road, then right to the entrance.
Information	Story County Conservation Board (515) 232-2516
County	Story

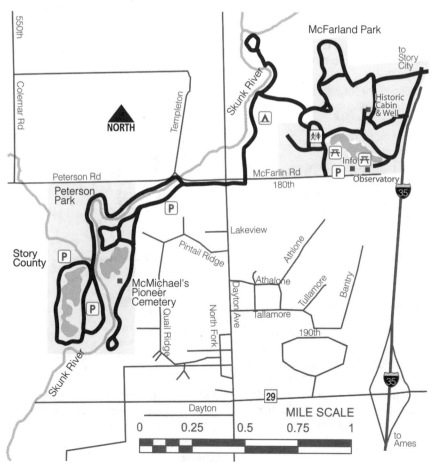

Des Moines Attractions

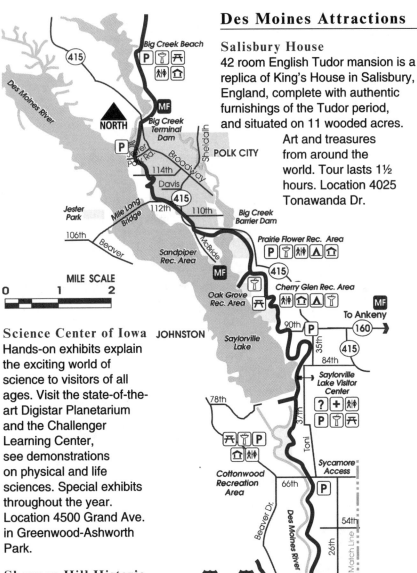

Salisbury House

42 room English Tudor mansion is a replica of King's House in Salisbury, England, complete with authentic furnishings of the Tudor period, and situated on 11 wooded acres. Art and treasures from around the world. Tour lasts 1½ hours. Location 4025 Tonawanda Dr.

Science Center of Iowa

Hands-on exhibits explain the exciting world of science to visitors of all ages. Visit the state-of-the-art Digistar Planetarium and the Challenger Learning Center, see demonstrations on physical and life sciences. Special exhibits throughout the year. Location 4500 Grand Ave. in Greenwood-Ashworth Park.

Sherman Hill Historic District

Elegant apartments, stately mansions and simple cottages from Victorian era and early 1900's in various stages of restoration. Group tours available. Self-guided tour brochure available at Wallace House. Annual fall house tour in September; winter tour first weekend in December. Location 756 16th St.

White Water University Waterpark

Wave pool, tubing rides, waterslides, lazy river and children's play pool. 18 hole mini golf, twin engine go-karts on an over/under track. Location 5401 E. University.

Neal Smith Trail
John Pat Dorrian Trail
Trestle to Trestle Trail

Trail Length	34.0 miles	Neal Smith – 26 miles John Pat Dorrian – 2.2 miles Trestle to Trestle Trail – 3.8 miles
Surface	Asphalt	
Vicinity	Des Moines, Polk City	
Location & Setting	The Saylorville-Des Moines River Trail follows the Des Moines River from the Birdland Marina in Des Moines, past Polk City to Big Creek Beach. The trail offers a variety of scenic vistas, including the Des Moines River Valley, Saylorville Lake, Big Creek Lake, prairies, ponds and forests. The upper segments provide rugged hills and valleys, while below Saylorville Dam, the grade is gently sloping.	
Information	Neal Smith Trail	(515) 276-4656
County	Polk	

ROUTE SLIP	INTERVAL	TOTAL
Hwy. 69/65		
Birdland Marina		1.2
McHenry Park	1.5	2.7
Euclid Ave.	1.5	4.2
Sycamore Access	4.8	9.0
Cottonwood Rec. Area	1.4	10.7
Saylorville Lake VC	1.1	11.5
NW 90th Pl.	2.5	14.0
Cherry Glen Rec. Area	1.1	15.1
Prairie Flower Rec. Area	1.7	16.8
Sandpiper Rec. Area	1.1	17.9
Jester Park Dr.	2.7	20.6
Big Creek	1.4	22.0
Big Creek Beach	4.0	26.0

State Capitol Building

Century-old building features a 275 foot gold-leafed dome flanked by four smaller domes. Inside, see legislative and Supreme Court chambers, governor's office, two-story law library and other state offices. Grand staircase and beautiful woodwork as well as other exhibits. Tours last 40 minutes. Capitol grounds include gardens, sculptures, fountains and monuments. Location E. Ninth & Grand Ave.

Trestle to Trestle Trail

McHenry Park

Drake University

University Ave.

Drake Park

DES MOINES

Aurora

Euclid

Birdland Park/Mari

Crocker-Woods Park

Nine Eagles State Park

Trail Length	7.0 miles of multi-use
Surface	Natural, groomed
Vicinity	Davis City
Location & Setting	Rugged wooded hills and valleys abundant with oak trees make Nine Eagles one of Iowa's most scenic parks. Facilities include picnic areas, shelters, campgrounds, and swimming beaches. Only rowboats and electric motors are permitted on the 64-acre lake. Lemoni is located 7 miles west of the park on Hwy 69, Davis City is 5.5 miles northwest, Pleasantton is 1 mile south, and Leon is 8 miles north on Hwy 69.
Information	Nines Eagles State Park (641) 442-2855
County	Decatur

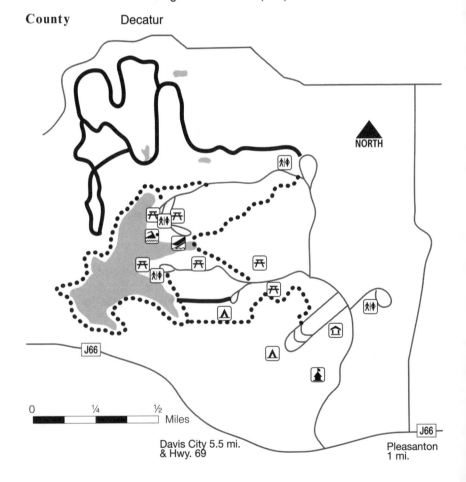

Old Creamery Trail

Trail Length	15.0 miles
Surface	Crushed limestone
Vicinity	Vinton, Dysart
Location & Setting	A planned 15-mile trail with 8-miles completed between Vinton and a mile beyond Garrison, a another 3-miles completed east of Dysart. The trail parallels Hinkle Creek and will extend to Dysart on a former railroad corridor. Setting is open and farmland.
Information	Iowa Trails Council (319) 849-1844
County	Benton

Pilot Knob State Park

Trail Length	8.0 miles
Surface	Natural, groomed
Vicinity	Forest City
Location & Setting	A 700-acre park located 4 miles from Forest City, and 12 south of Rice Lake State Park, in north central Iowa. The tower on Pilot Knob is the second highest point in the state, and provides a spectacular view. Facilities include restrooms, picnic areas, shelters, a playground, 60 campsites, and an open-air amphitheater. Hidden in the park and unique in Iowa is a 4-acre floating sphagnum bog, called Dead Man's Lake. There is also a 15-acre man-made lake available for electric motor boating, fishing and ice skating in winter.
Information	Pilot Knob State Park (641) 581-4835
County	Winnebago, Hancock

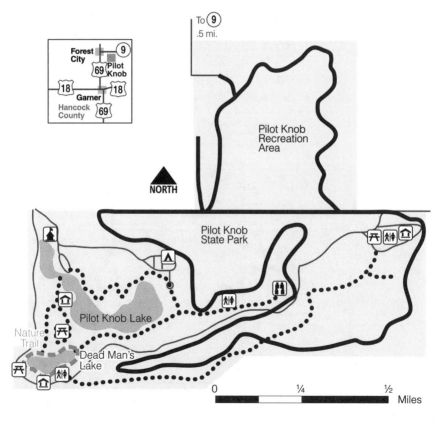

Pine Lake State Park

Trail Length	7.5 miles
Surface	Paved, crushed stone, dirt, grass
Vicinity	Eldora, Steamboat Rock
Location & Setting	The 585-acre park provides a mix of woodland, river, and lake in the midst of rolling farmland. The bike trail consists of the 2.5-mile concrete surfaced trail within the park and the 2.5-mile asphalt trail paralleling Hwy 56 to Steamboat Rock. The 2.5-mile multi-use trail has a combination surface of dirt, grass, and crushed stone. The 1.5-mile hiking trail is not open to bicycling.
Information	Pine Lake State Park (641) 858-5832
County	Hardin

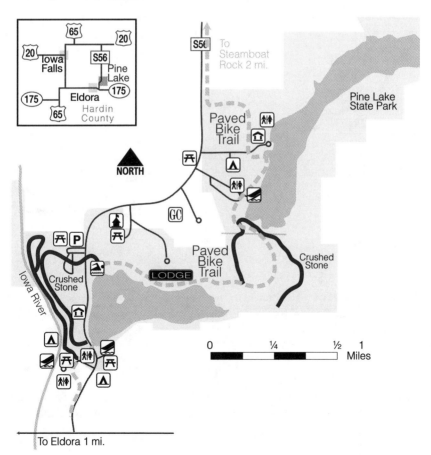

Pioneer Trail

Trail Length	12.0 miles
Surface	Crushed limestone (plus grass surface for equestrian use)
Vicinity	Reinbeck, Grundy Center
Location & Setting	The trail is a link in the American Discovery Trail between Reinbeck and Holland in northeastern Iowa. Built largely on abandoned rail bed. Open areas, farmland, some wooded area, small communities.
Information	Grundy County Conservation Board (319) 345-2688
County	Grundy

The Pioneer Trail was named in recognition of the pioneers who settled in the area in the 1850's.

Currently there is no public access between Grundy Center and just west of Reinbeck.

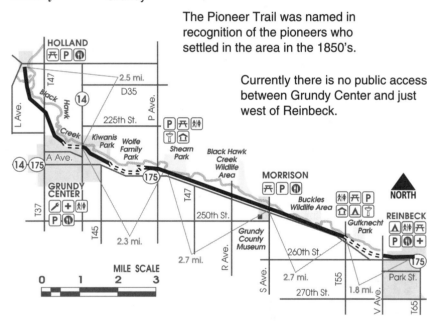

Grundy Center Attractions

Herbert Quick Schoolhouse One room county schoolhouse where noted Iowa author and publisher Herbert Quick attended school. Furnished with original items. Location Hwys 175 and 14.

Morrison Attractions

Grundy County Museum 1912 schoolhouse with historical, natural history and railroad displays, restored and furnished log cabin. Location 203 3rd St.

Black Hawk Creek Wildlife Area Swinging suspension bridge Location ¼ mile north of Morrison on County Road T-53.

Pleasant Creek State Recreation Area

Trail Length	10.0 miles
Surface	Packed dirt and grass
Vicinity	Center Point, Shellsburg
Location & Setting	Effort level is easy to moderate. The setting is wooded with open areas. The south section is mostly hilly. Camping and swimming facilities are available. Entrances off of W36 about 5-miles south of Center Point, and 4-miles north of Palo.
Information	Pleasant Creek State Recreation Area (319) 436-7716
County	Benton, Lynn

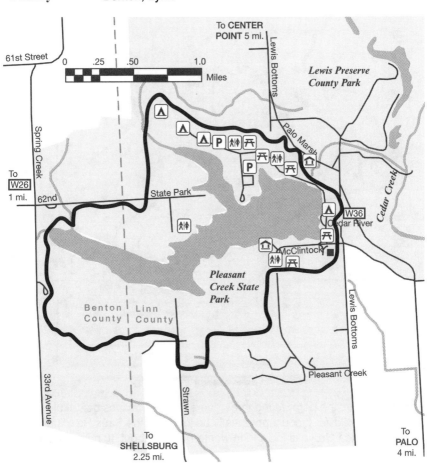

Pleasant Valley Trail

Trail Length	4.5 miles
Surface	Concrete
Vicinity	Ida Grove
Location & Setting	Ida Grove. The trail is constructed on flood control right-of-way and runs from the high school and then follows Badger Creek, and along Maple River and Odebolt Creek, then back to the high school, forming a loop.
Information	City of Ida Grove (712) 364-2428
County	Ida

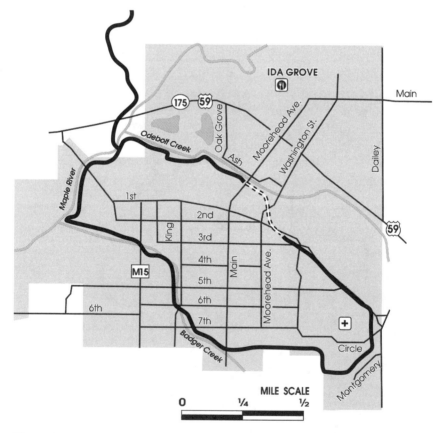

The trail utilizes the berm along three rivers, which provides beautiful scenery and wildlife. It could potentially be joined to the Sauk Rail Trail in Sac County. Ida Grove is located in western Iowa, about 40 miles east of Sioux City.

Pony Hollow Trail

Trail Length	4.0 miles
Surface	Crushed stone
Vicinity	Elkader
Location & Setting	Town of Elkader in northeast Iowa. The trail forms a 'U' with the southwest trailhead commencing on the east side of Hwy. 13 and the north trailhead on the south side of Hwy 128.
Information	Clayton County Conservation Board (563) 245-1516
County	Clayton

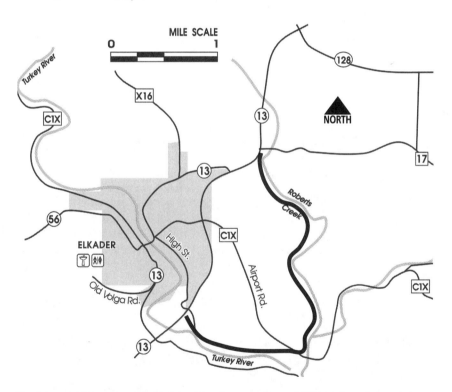

Restroom, showers and electrical hook ups are available at the city park in Elkader. The Osborne Conservation Center is five miles south of Elkader on Hwy 13. It includes an Iowa Welcome Center, nature center, primitive campground, plus four hiking trails.

A state fish hatchery is located just north west of Elkader.

Praeri Rail Trail

Trail Length   10.5 miles

Surface   Crushed limestone, mowed grass

Vicinity   Roland, Zearing

Location & Setting   Built on abandoned railbed, this trail corridor runs from Roland through McCallsburg to Zearing in central Iowa. The trail parallels Hwy E18.

Information   Story County Conservation Board   (515) 232-2516

County   Story

The spelling of the work "Praeri" is in recognition of the area's strong Norwegian heritage.

Park hours are 5 a.m. to 10:30 p.m. Many segments of native prairie remnants can be seen adjacent to the trail.

Nearby Attractions Ames

Octagon Center for the Arts Changing exhibits and large museum gift shop. Location 427 Douglas.

Farm House Museum Built in the 1860's, the first building at IA State Agricultural College & Model Farm. Over 6,000 pieces of Victorian decorative arts & antique furnishings. Location 290 Scheman.

Reiman Gardens Wetland garden, entry courtyard, herb garden, rose garden and collections such as peonies, daylilies, iris. Annual garden flowers throughout the garden. The Education Center will offer workshops and meetings. Location Elwood Dr.; main entrance to campus from Hwy 30.

Brunnier Art Museum National and international art exhibitions, collections of glass, ceramics and art from Eastern and Western cultures, gallery talks, children's programs. Location 290 Scheman.

Prairie Farmer Recreation Trail

Trail Length	20.0 miles
Surface	Crushed limestone (scheduled for paving by end of 2008)
Vicinity	Calmar, Cresco
Location & Setting	The trail is built on the abandoned Milwaukee Railroad line between Calmer and Cresco The setting includes native prairie, wooded areas and farmland.
Information	Winneshiek County Conservation Board (563) 534-7145
County	Winneshiek

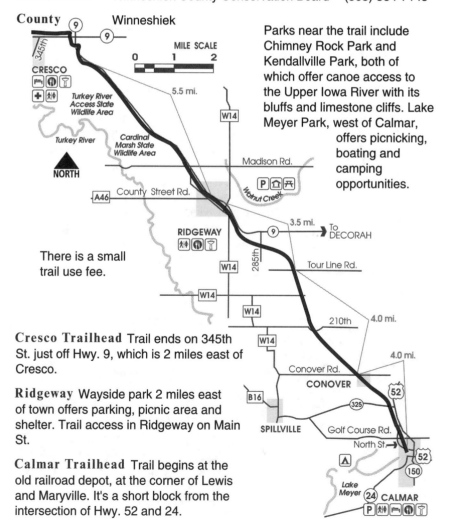

Parks near the trail include Chimney Rock Park and Kendallville Park, both of which offer canoe access to the Upper Iowa River with its bluffs and limestone cliffs. Lake Meyer Park, west of Calmar, offers picnicking, boating and camping opportunities.

There is a small trail use fee.

Cresco Trailhead Trail ends on 345th St. just off Hwy. 9, which is 2 miles east of Cresco.

Ridgeway Wayside park 2 miles east of town offers parking, picnic area and shelter. Trail access in Ridgeway on Main St.

Calmar Trailhead Trail begins at the old railroad depot, at the corner of Lewis and Maryville. It's a short block from the intersection of Hwy. 52 and 24.

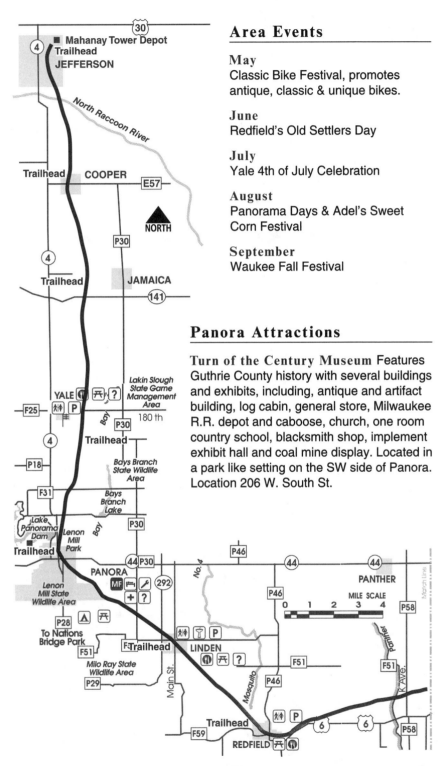

Area Events

May
Classic Bike Festival, promotes antique, classic & unique bikes.

June
Redfield's Old Settlers Day

July
Yale 4th of July Celebration

August
Panorama Days & Adel's Sweet Corn Festival

September
Waukee Fall Festival

Panora Attractions

Turn of the Century Museum Features Guthrie County history with several buildings and exhibits, including, antique and artifact building, log cabin, general store, Milwaukee R.R. depot and caboose, church, one room country school, blacksmith shop, implement exhibit hall and coal mine display. Located in a park like setting on the SW side of Panora. Location 206 W. South St.

Raccoon River Valley Trail

Trail Length	56.0 miles
Surface	Asphalt, some concrete
Vicinity	Jefferson, Panora, Waukee
Location & Setting	Located northwest of Des Moines between Waukee and Jefferson, winding through the Raccoon River Greenbelt. Enjoy the prairie remnants, bottom land timber, wildlife habitat, and the opportunity to tour several communities without leaving the trail. It will be extended south to Clive, and is a link in the American Discovery Trail.
Information	Dallas County Conservation Dept. (515) 465-3577 Guthrie County Conservation Board (641) 755-3061
County	Dallas, Guthrie

Trees line much of this asphalt trail, sometimes creating a canopy effect.

ROUTE SLIP	INTERVAL	TOTAL
Hwy 80/35	.0	
Waukee	5.0	5.0
Adel	6.0	11.0
Redfield	10.0	21.0
Linden	6.0	27.0
Panora	6.0	33.0
Yale	6.0	39.0
Herndon	5.0	44.0
Cooper	5.0	49.0
Jefferson	7.0	56.0

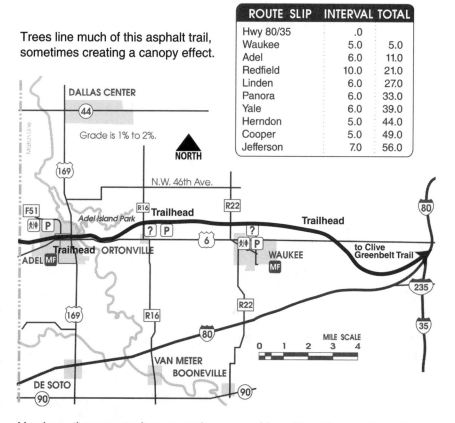

You have the opportunity to tour six communities without leaving the trail, plus enjoy the prairie remnants, bottom land timber and wildlife habitat.

Trolley Trail
River City Trail
Winnebago Trail

Trail Length	Total	17.5 miles
	River City Trail	8.5 miles
	Trolley Trail	5.0 miles
	Winnebago Trail	2.0 miles
	NIACC Extension	2.0 miles

Surface	River City Trail streets	paved, crushed limestone, city
	Trolley Trail	asphalt
	Winnebago Trail	crushed limestone

Vicinity   Mason City, Clear Lake

Location & Setting   Mason City in north central Iowa. There are trailheads with parking at Milligan Park, at Elm and 13th Street and at Lime Creek Nature Center.

Information   Cerro Gordo County Conservation Board   (641) 423-5309

County   Cerro Gordo

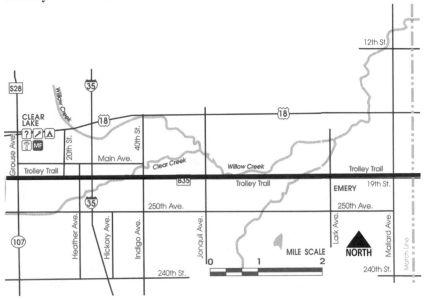

TRAIL USES LEGEND

- 🚲 Leisure Biking
- 🚵 Mountain Biking
- 🚶 Hiking
- ⛷ Cross-country Skiing
- 🐴 Horseback Riding
- 🛼 Rollerblading
- 🛷 Other

TRAIL LEGEND

———————	Bike/Multi Trail
••••••••••	Hiking only Trail
▬▬▬▬▬▬	XC Skiing only
==========	Planned Trail
▬ ▬ ▬ ▬ ▬	Alternate Trail
———————	Road/Highway
┼┼┼┼┼┼┼┼	Railroad Tracks

The River City Trail links Milligan and East Parks with cultural attractions of Mason City and its downtown areas. It follows along an abandoned railroad bed, parks and city streets. The downtown Riverwalk Trail is lighted. The Winnebago Trail proceeds north along the Winnebago River to the Lime Creek Nature Center. It offers picturesque views of the river's limestone bluffs as it transverses meadow and woods.

The Trolley Trail connects Mason City and Clear Lake. It runs parallel to County Road B35 and Mason City's electric trolley line which operates between the two cities. This is America's last working electric trolley.

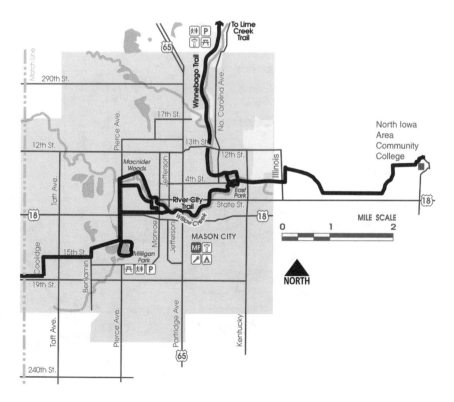

Rock Creek State Park

Trail Length	14.0 miles
Surface	Natural – grass, rocks
Vicinity	Grinnell, Kellogg
Location & Setting	Rock Creek State Park is located 5 miles northeast of Kellogg and 6 miles west of Grinnell in central Iowa. The trailhead is on the west side of the Rock Creek beach parking lot. Effort level is generally moderate and singletrack. Facilities include picnic areas, shelter, a large campground with electrical hookups, modern rest rooms and showers, a swimming beach, and boating.
Information	Rock Creek State Park (641) 236-3722
County	Jasper

14
14 F27
6
80 80
Rock Creek
Newton
14
Jasper County

NORTH

To Hwy. 138 3 mi.
& Grinnell 6 mi.

F27

F27

To Hwy. 224 & Kellogg

0   ¼   ½   1
Miles

To 6

Rock Island
Old Stone Arch

Trail Length	4.0 miles
Surface	Asphalt - 10 feet wide
Vicinity	Shelby
Location & Setting	The trail begins in Shelby on the south at Hwy I-80, exit #34 and follows the former Chicago, Rock Island & Pacific line to a 6 acre timber area in southwest rural Shelby County. The city of Shelby is 20 miles northeast of Council Bluffs.
Information	City of Shelby (712) 544-2404
County	Shelby

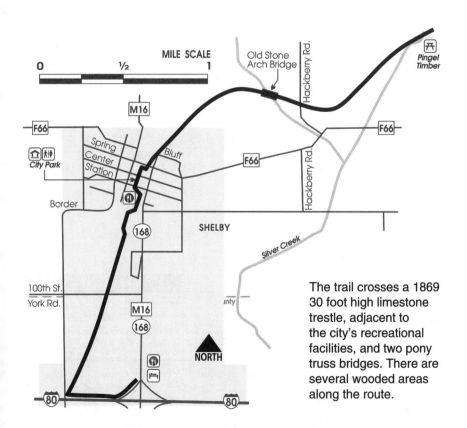

The trail crosses a 1869 30 foot high limestone trestle, adjacent to the city's recreational facilities, and two pony truss bridges. There are several wooded areas along the route.

Rolling Prairie Trail
Butler County Nature Trail
Waverly Rail Trail
Denver-Jefferson Trail

Trail Length	20.5 miles, over 60 miles when completed
Surface	Asphalt
Vicinity	Allison, Clarksville, Denver, Shell Rock
Location & Setting	The Rolling Prairie Trail System is being developed on former railroad bed, and will span a three county area when completed. The Rolling Prairie Trail is 6 miles in length and runs from Allison to Clarksville. It is paved into Henry Woods State Park at Clarksville. The Butler County Nature Trail is 5.5 miles in length and runs from Clarksville to Shell Rock. The trail currently ends a mile east of Clarksville where riders use a bike lane along C33. The Waverly Rail Trail runs for 7 miles from Waverly to Hwy 63. The Denver-Jefferson Trail continues from Hwy 63 for 2 miles to Denver. The trail system will eventually be extended both east and west to Readlyn on the "Grump Trail" and to Coulter from Allison on the newly acquired railroad right of way. Readlyn advertises its slogan as "785 friendly residents and one old grump."

Currently there are trailheads at Allison, Clarksville, Shell Rock, Waverly, and Denver. |
| **Information** | Rolling Prairie Trail Committee   (319) 267-2858 |
| **County** | Bremer, Butler, Franklin |

TRAIL LEGEND	
——	Bike/Multi Trail
••••••••••	Hiking only Trail
▪▪▪▪▪▪▪▪▪▪	XC Skiing only
==========	Planned Trail
≈ ≈ ≈ ≈ ≈ ≈	Alternate Trail
——	Road/Highway
++++++++++	Railroad Tracks

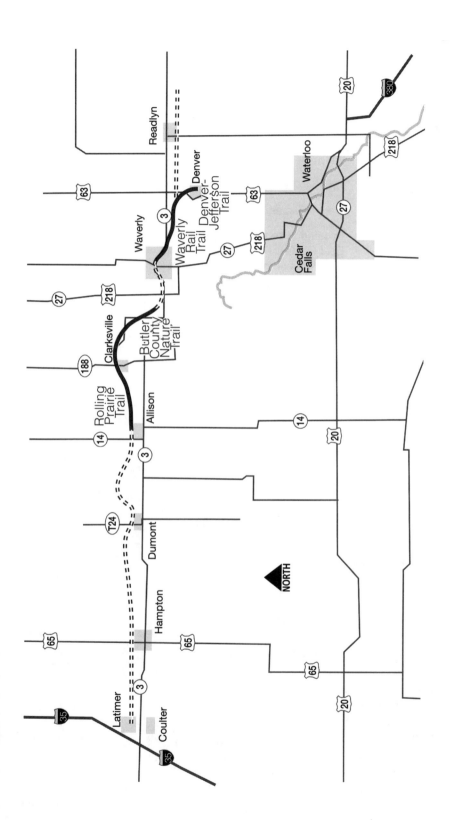

Sac & Fox Recreation Trail

Trail Length	7.5 miles
Surface	Crushed Limestone
Vicinity	Cedar Rapids
Location & Setting	Located in south east Cedar Rapids from Cole Street to East Post Road. It runs through a deep forest valley for about half of the trail. The rest of the trail follows the Cedar River and is in more open terrain.
Information	Indian Creek Nature Center (319) 362-0664
County	Linn

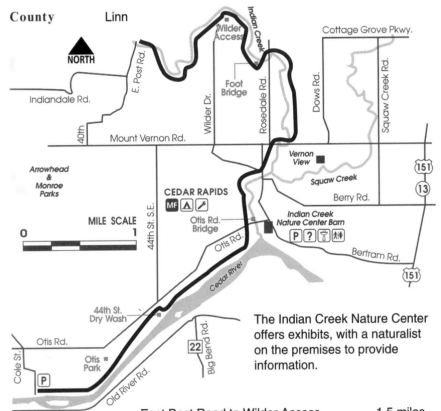

The Indian Creek Nature Center offers exhibits, with a naturalist on the premises to provide information.

There is an admission charge to the Indian Creek Nature Center for non-members.

East Post Road to Wilder Access	1.5 miles
Wilder Access to Mt. Vernon Road	2.0 miles
Mt. Vernon Road to Otis Road Bridge	1.0 miles
Otis Rd. Bridge to 44th St. Dry Wash	1.5 miles
44th St. Dry Wash to Cole St. parking lot	1.5 miles
Total	**7.5 miles**

Scott County Park

Trail Length	5.0 miles	
Surface	Dirt, mowed grass	
Vicinity	Davenport	
Location & Setting	Located in easy central Iowa, the trail is looped, single-track, with a surface of dirt and mowed-grass. Effort level ranges from easy to difficult. The setting is wooded with open, grassy areas. Facilities include camping, a nature center, swimming, and a petting zoo.	
Information	Scott County Park	(563) 328-3282
County	Scott	

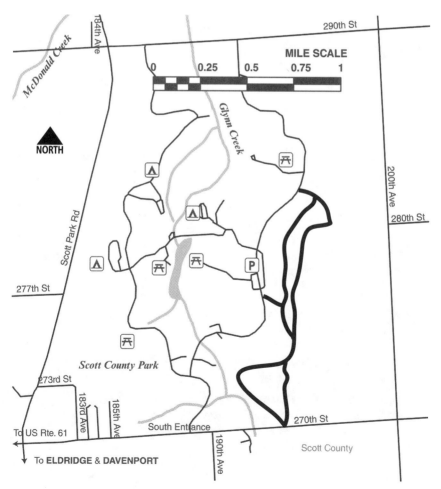

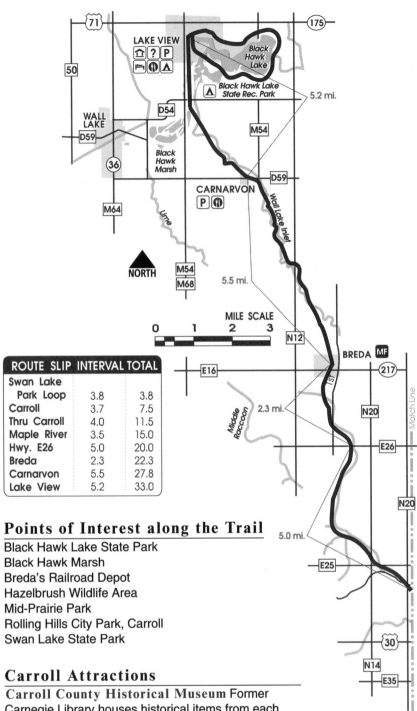

ROUTE SLIP	INTERVAL	TOTAL
Swan Lake Park Loop	3.8	3.8
Carroll	3.7	7.5
Thru Carroll	4.0	11.5
Maple River	3.5	15.0
Hwy. E26	5.0	20.0
Breda	2.3	22.3
Carnarvon	5.5	27.8
Lake View	5.2	33.0

Points of Interest along the Trail

Black Hawk Lake State Park
Black Hawk Marsh
Breda's Railroad Depot
Hazelbrush Wildlife Area
Mid-Prairie Park
Rolling Hills City Park, Carroll
Swan Lake State Park

Carroll Attractions

Carroll County Historical Museum Former
Carnegie Library houses historical items from each
town in Carroll County. Also visit Farmstead Museum
at Swan Lake, Log Cabin and Little Red Schoolhouse
in Graham Park. Location 123 E. 6th.

Sauk Rail Trail
Swan Lake Park

Trail Length	33.0 miles
Surface	Asphalt – Swan Lake to Maple River; Crushed limestone– Maple River to Carnarvon; Concrete – Carnarvon to Lakeview.
Vicinity	Carroll, Lake View
Location & Setting	West central Iowa between Carroll and Lake View. Built on abandoned Chicago Northwestern rail bed for 13 miles and a 50 foot right-of-way for 20 miles. The area consists of prairies, wetlands, farmland and woodlands. The Saul Rail Trail was the first rail trail in the nation converted under the terms of the NTSA.
Information	Carroll County Conservation Board (712) 792-4614 Sac County Conservation Board (712) 662-4530
County	Carroll, Sac

SWAN LAKE PARK

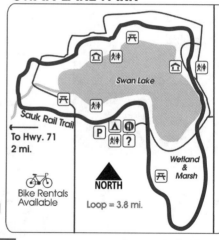

There is a small users fee for ages 12 and over.

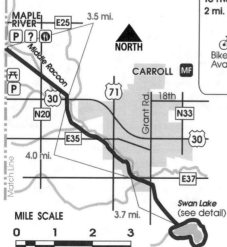

Points of Interest

Swan Lake State Park
Located 2.5 miles east of Carroll. A 510 acre multi-use area including bike and boat rentals, swimming, camping, picnicking, cross country skiing and snowmobiling.

Glacial Boulders in Iowa

This 67 lb. nugget of native copper, tinged with greenish oxides, is one of the most distinctive glacial erratics found in Iowa and probably originated from the lake Superior area along the Upper Peninsula of Michigan. (Specimen is 15 inches long and 9 inches wide.) Photo by Paul VanDorpe.

"Peculiar," "irregular," and "uncommon," are words used to describe one class of Iowa rocks—glacial boulders or "erratics." Geologists define erratics as stones or boulders that have been carried from their place of origin by a glacier and then left stranded by melting ice on bedrock of a different composition. In Iowa, glacial erratics are commonly observed where glacial deposits occur at the land surface, primarily in the north-central and northeastern parts of the state.

Glacial grooves and striations inscribe the limestone bedrock exposed in a Des Moines County quarry. These sets of parallel furrows and lines were gouged by glacial boulders embedded in the base of a slowly moving ice sheet. Photo by Holmes Semken

This Black Hawk County field strewn with glacial erratics is typical of many pastures on the Iowan Surface of northeastern Iowa. Photo by Pat Lohmann

In western and southern Iowa, erratics generally lie buried beneath wind-deposited silts (loess) that cover the glacial materials. In these areas, erratics generally are restricted to valleys, where streams have eroded through the loess and into the underlying glacial deposits.

A large, weathered and rounded boulder of granite in this circa 1900 photograph of a Mason City neighborhood is a monument to the massive glacier that brought it south over 500,000 years ago. The nearest bedrock source of this erratic is central Minnesota. Photo courtesy of The University of Iowa Calvin Collection.

Excerpts by Raymond R. Anderson and Jean Cutler Prior Adapted from Iowa Geology 1990, No. 15, Iowa Department of Natural Resources

Shimek Forest Trail

Trail Length	27 miles
Surface	Natural, groomed
Vicinity	Farmington
Location & Setting	Shimek State Forest consists of over 8,900 acres and is located east of Farmington in the southeast corner of Iowa. The trail is an abandoned railbed and can be accessed by exiting right on an old forest logging road, off road J58, northeast of Farmington.
Information	Shimek State Forest (319) 878-3811
County	Van Buren, Lee

Check with the Forest Headquarters located north off J56 a short distance out of Farmington to determine alternate mountain biking opportunities in the Forest and nearby areas.

Shimek State Forest

Croton Rd.

250th St.

Croton Civil War Memorial Park

Croton

Des Moines River

J62

255th St.

Belfast Rd.

W62

Croton Rd.

NORTH

0	¼	½	1
Miles

Sioux City Area Trails

Trail Length	45 miles
Surface	Paved
Vicinity	Sioux City
Location & Setting	Sioux City is located in northwest Iowa and borders both Nebraska and South Dakota across the Missouri River. The city offers a variety of bike trails, providing opportunities to enjoy the sights seen along the pathways. The trails are open from 7 am to 11 pm.
Information	Siouxland Interstate Parks & Recreation (712) 233-3240
County	Woodbury

Sioux City Attractions

Sergeant Floyd Riverboat Museum and Welcome Center Diesel inspection ship plied the Missouri River for 50 years as the flagship of the U.S. Army Corps of Engineers construction fleet. See the history of Missouri River transportation through rare photos, artifacts, dioramas and America's largest display of scale Missouri River steamboat and keelboat models, and Iowa's only professional model ship building shop. Special focus on the 1804 Lewis & Clark Expedition. Location 1000 Larson Park Rd. / Exit 149 on I-29.

Sioux City Public Museum Built from pink colored Sioux Falls quartzite in the early 1890's, the Pierce mansion exhibits pioneer materials from antique needlework to a finished log cabin interior. Explore the natural history of the area through displays of birds, fish, animals and minerals. Indian artifacts displayed. Location 2901 Jackson St.

SHRA Railroad Museum Traces the history of the area's railroad industry. Photos, artifacts, large HO-scale model. Tours of railroad caboose and 1943 locomotive. Gift shop with railroad merchandise. Location 2001 Leech Ave.

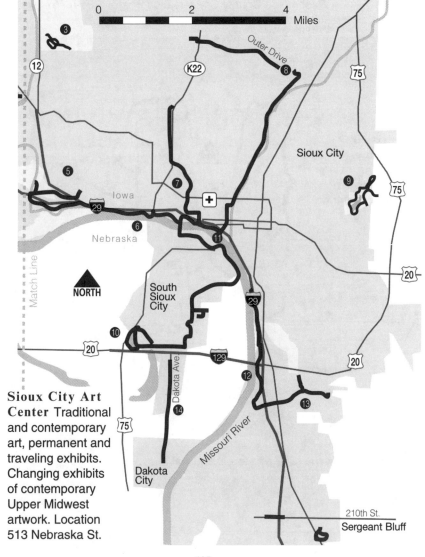

Trails		Miles	Surface	
❶	Adams Homestead & NP	3.0	Stone	Ⓟ 🚶
❷	McCook Lake Trail	4.0	Paved	
❸	Stone State Prk	5.0	Natural	Ⓟ 🚶
❹	Dakota Dunes Trail		Under development	
❺	Lewis & Clark Trail	6.0	Paved	Ⓟ 🚶
❻	Perry Creek Trail		Under development	
❼	Floyd River Trail	3.0	Paved	Ⓟ
❽	Bacon Creek Trail	4.4	Paved	Ⓟ 🚶
❾	Crystal Cove Trail	1.5	Paved	Ⓟ 🚶
❿	Al Bengston Trail	6.6	Paved	Ⓟ 🚶
⓫	Chautauqua Park Trail	2.7	Paved	Ⓟ
⓬	Singing Hills Trail	2.0	Paved	Ⓟ
⓭	Dakota City Trail	2.0	Paved	Ⓟ

Sioux City Art Center Traditional and contemporary art, permanent and traveling exhibits. Changing exhibits of contemporary Upper Midwest artwork. Location 513 Nebraska St.

Sockum Ridge Park

Trail Length	10.0 miles (approx)
Surface	Grass, dirt
Vicinity	Washington
Location & Setting	A 215-acre managed woodland of upland timber. The canopy is dominated by red and white oak. The park is located 5-miles southeast of Washington. From W55 (Wayland Rd.), take 305th Street east for a half mile.
Information	Washington County Conversation Board (319) 657-2400
County	Washington

Park facilities include: Parking, toilets and canoeing, but no water or camping.

Sockum Ridge Park is hilly, with forest and wetlands.

Spencer Recreational Trail

Trail Length	9.0 miles
Surface	Paved
Vicinity	Spencer
Location & Setting	The trail system meanders through Spencer offering some 9 miles of multi-use trails. The paved trail encircles Stolley Park, known for its beautiful nature area. It continues through East Leach Park, and includes a bridge over the Little Sioux River, connecting the park to southeast Spencer.
Information	Spencer Parks Dept. (712) 580-7260
County	Clay

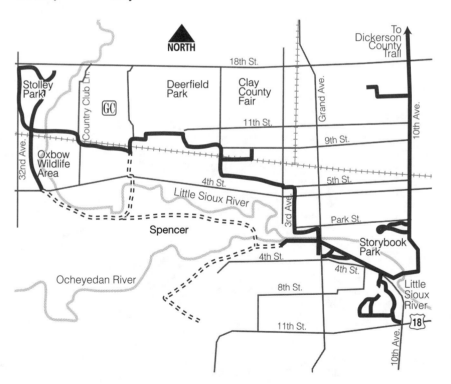

Squaw Creek Park

Trail Length	4.0 miles
Surface	Natural, groomed
Vicinity	Marion
Location & Setting	The park is located southeast of Marion. The 4 mile multi-use, groomed trail winds through open meadows, woods, and brushy creek bottoms. Effort level is easy to moderate. There is an all-weather lodge open for day use.
Information	Linn County Conservation Board (319) 398-6450
County	Linn

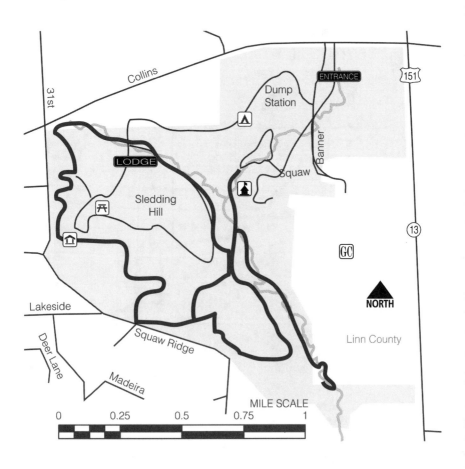

Stone State Park

Trail Length   10.0 miles (6 miles open to bicycling)

Surface   Natural

Vicinity   Sioux City

Location & Setting   Located in the northwest corner of Sioux City with 1,085 acres in Woodbury and Plymouth Counties. The Park can be accessed from Talbot Road off Memorial Drive.

Information   Stone State Park   (712) 255-4698

County   Woodbury, Plymouth

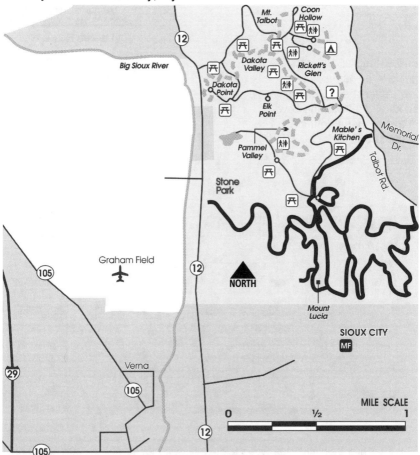

In addition to the trail system, park facilities include a lodge, and camping and picnic area. Stone Park is located entirely in the unique Loess Hills of western Iowa. These hills were formed many thousands of years ago by windblown soil.

Storm Lake LakeTrail

Trail Length	5.0 miles
Surface	Concrete, plus sidewalks and low traffic streets.
Vicinity	Storm Lake
Location & Setting	Storm Lake in northwestern Iowa. The trail follows the north side of Storm Lake connecting the village of Lakeside at the east end with Emerald Park at the west end.
Information	Storm Lake Parks and Recreation Dept. (712) 732-8027
County	Buena Vista

Follow the trail signs to guide your way along the low-traffic streets. Bikers should travel with the flow of traffic on the right side of the street.

TRAIL USES LEGEND
- Leisure Biking
- Mountain Biking
- Hiking
- Cross-country Skiing
- Horseback Riding
- Rollerblading
- Other

The five-mile trail links pathways, sidewalks and low-traffic streets and runs through recreation, historic and residential areas. Facilities at the parks include picnic areas, water sports and playgrounds.

Sugar Bottom Recreation Area

Trail Length	10.0 miles
Surface	Natural
Vicinity	North Liberty
Location & Setting	The trail consists of a series of loops, single track and one-way. Effort level ranges from easy to fairly difficult. The setting is mostly wooded, with some open areas. Services include a campground, water and restrooms. From North Liberty, northeast on F28 to the park entrance, with access to the trail from the Day Use area.
Information	U.S. Army Corps of Engineers (319) 338-3543
County	Johnson

Mehaffey Bridge

MILE SCALE

0   0.25   0.5

Hiland View

Broganville

Johnson County

Sugar Bottom

NORTH

Fast Times

Thorn

The Old Trail

Access Road

Hell Trail

Coralville Lake

Summerset Trail

Trail Length	11.0 miles
Surface	Asphalt
Vicinity	Carlisle, Indianola
Location & Setting	Built on converted rail bed, running between Carisle and Indianola south of Des Moines. Setting includes farmland, woods north of Indianola and wetlands between Summerset and Carlisle. Open between sunrise and sunset. Carisle access is off Rte 5, and the Indianola trailhead is off 5th St., a block east of Hwy 65/19.
Information	Warren County Conservation Board (515) 961-6169
County	Warren

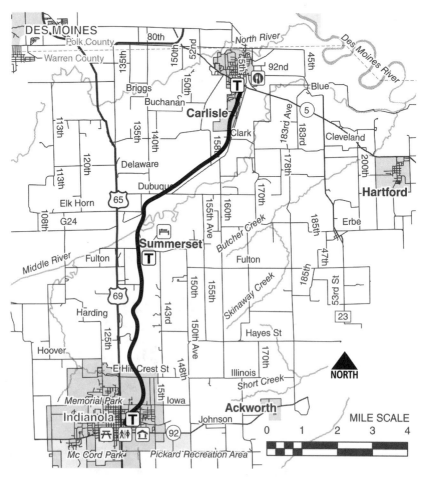

T-Bone Trail

Trail Length	21 miles (approx. 16 miles complete)
Surface	Asphalt
Vicinity	Audubon, Atlantic
Location & Setting	The T-Bone Trail largely parallels Hwy. 71 between Audubon in Audubon County and Atlantic in Cass County. It is developed on abandoned rail-grade.
Information	Audubon County Conservation Board (712) 268-2762
County	Audubon, Cass

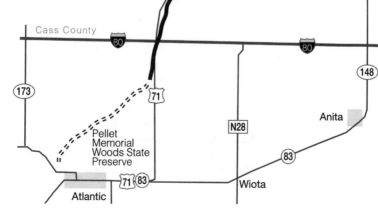

Three Rivers Trail

Trail Length	33.0 miles (total of 44 miles when complete), plus a spur running south of Humboldt to Gotch State Park
Surface	Crushed limestone (10 feet wide)
Vicinity	Eagle Grove, Humboldt, Rolfe
Location & Setting	North central Iowa, built on abandoned railbed and running between the communities of Eagle Grove in Wright County through Humboldt County to Rolfe in Pocahontas County.
Information	Humboldt County Conservation Board (515) 332-4087
Counties	Humboldt, Pocahontas, Wright

Trail amenities include shelter houses, restrooms, access parking lots and picnic areas along the route.

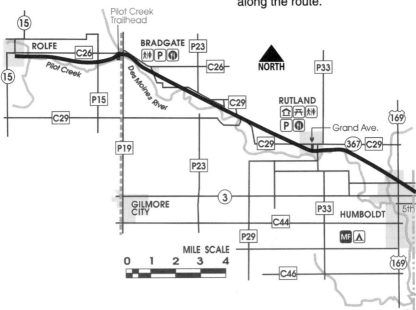

As the name implies, the trail crosses three rivers - the east fork of the Des Moines River, the west fork of the Des Moines River, and the Boone River. The western portion travels through beautiful timber with many scenic views of the west branch of the Des Moines River.

Nearby Parks With Facilities

Frank A. Gotch Park 4 miles south of Humboldt on Hwy 169. 1 mile east and 2 miles north. 67 acres with campsites, canoeing, fishing, boat ramp, showers, shelter, playground.

Humboldt Izaak Walton Park 1.5 miles west of Humboldt on Hwy 3. Features picnic areas, boat ramp, playground, fishing.

Lotts Creek Area ½ mile west of Livermore on 130th. A 30 acre park featuring campsites, picnic, wildlife area.

Oakdale Park 2.5 miles south and 1.5 miles east of Renwick. Features shelters, restroom, water, electric, picnic.

Joe Sheldon Park 1.75 miles west of Humboldt on Hwy 3. An 81 acre park featuring campsites, fishing, boat ramp, electric, showers, playgrounds, shelters.

Mileage Increments	Miles
Eagle Grove to Humboldt County Line	3.0
County Line to P66	2.1
P66 to Long Tree Road	6.7
Lone Tree Road to 5 Street (Dakota City)	2.6
5 Street to Hwy 169 (Dakota City)	1.7
Hwy 169 to Grand Ave. (Rutland)	3.6
Grand Ave. to Saturn's (Bradgate)	7.4
Saturn's to Pilot Creek	0.7
Pilot Creek to Rolfe	5.2
Total	**33.0**
Spur from Humboldt to Gotch Park	6.0

The eastern portion of the trail passes through shrubby grasslands, marshy areas and open prairie. The trail has an abundance of remnant prairie sites with many species of wild flowers and grasses.

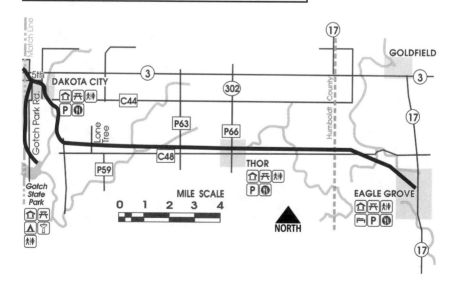

Volga River State Recreation Area

Trail Length	25 miles
Surface	Natural
Vicinity	Fayette
Location & Setting	Two miles northeast of Fayette in northeast Iowa. The west entrance is one mile east of Hwy. 150 and the east entrance is 4 miles west of Wadena.
Information	Volga River State Recreation Area (563) 425-4161
County	Fayette

Fossils of Iowa

Some of these fossils can be found in or near river banks, quarries and other areas throughout Iowa.

Bryozoan

Solitary Coral

Seed Fern Leaves

Scale Tree Trunk

Crinoid

Stromatoporoid

Gastropod

Courtesy of Iowa Dept. of Natural Resources

Located 4 miles north of Fayette in scenic northern Iowa on the meandering Volga River. Site features campground with basic facilities and specified campsites.

Elevation : 500 ft.

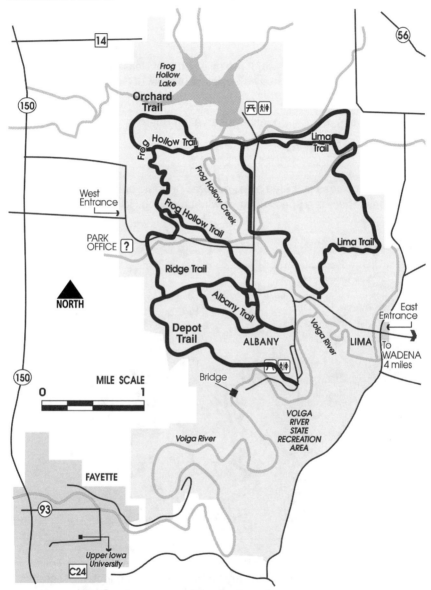

The park has 5,459 acres. The general area is often referred to as "Little Switzerland" because of its rugged topography, geologic features and substantial woods. The self-guided nature trail begins by the park office at the west entrance. Red fox, raccoon, skunk, opossum, muskrat, mine, beaver, white-tailed deer and wild turkey are all found in the area.

Volksweg Trail

Trail Length	13.0 miles
Surface	Asphalt
Vicinity	Pella
Location & Setting	Central Iowa, three mile south of Pella, which is approximately 45 miles southeast of Des Moines on Hwy 163.
Information	Marion County Conservation Board (641) 828-2213
County	Marion

The setting includes timbered area, restored prairies, open fields and pine plantations. There is a spectacular view of Lake Red Rock.

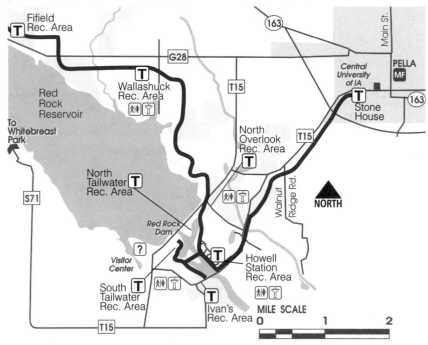

Volksweg is a Dutch word meaning "people's path". The Volksweg Trail is an asphalt paved trail with width varying from eight to ten feet. Most grades along the trail are less than 5%. However a few approach 7%. The section running from the North Tailwater Recreation Area to the Howell Station Recreation Area has a slope of less than 1%. The trail section connecting the city of Pella to the recreational areas of Lake Red Rock runs parallel to County Road T-15.

Wapsi-Great Western Line

Trail Length	12.0 miles (will be 22.0 miles when completed), plus 2 miles surrounding Lake Hendricks.
Surface	Crushed limestone (trail segment surrounding Lake Hendricks is mowed grass).
Vicinity	Riceville
Location & Setting	Northeastern Iowa, extending north from Riceville. Straddles Howard and Mitchell Counties.
Information	Mitchell County Conservation Board (641) 732-5204
County	Howard, Mitchell

The Wapsi-Great Western Line runs both on the Wapsipinicon River corridor and abandoned railbed. The trail traverses hilltops and rolling landscapes, native prairie and timber areas. The addition planned will add a large loop at the north end.

There is a butterfly garden built into a hillside along the trail.

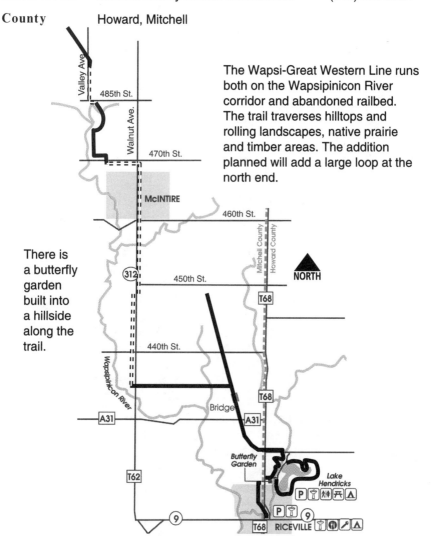

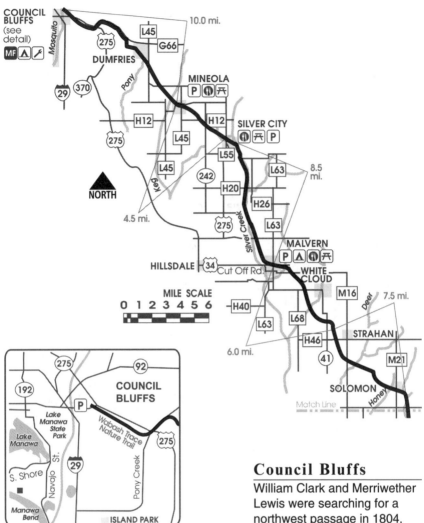

Points of Interest:

Bellevue, NE	Fontenelle Forest Nature Center
Council Bluffs	Lewis & Clark Monument General Dodge House Squirrel Cage Jail
Honey Creek	Hitchcock Nature Center
Malvern	Railroad Depot
Omaha, NE	Western Heritage Museum
Shenandoah	Restored Wabash Depot

Council Bluffs

William Clark and Merriwether Lewis were searching for a northwest passage in 1804, when they met for a council with the Otoe and Missouri Indians on a bluff overlooking the Missouri River, hence the name "Council Bluffs".

ROUTE SLIP	INTERVAL	TOTAL
Council Bluffs		
Mineola	10.0	10.0
Silver City	4.5	14.5
Malvern	8.5	23.0
Imogene	13.5	36.5
Shenandoah	8.5	45.0
Izaak Walton Lodge	5.0	50.0
Coin	7.5	57.5
Blanchard	5.5	63.0

Wabash Trace Nature Trail

Trail Length	64.5 miles
Surface	Limestone screenings, with two miles of asphalt in Shenandoah
Vicinity	Council Bluffs, Shenandoah, Blanchard
Location & Setting	The Wabash Trace, located in southwest Iowa, is built on an abandoned rail bed and runs from Council Bluffs to Blanchard at the Missouri state line. The trail is frequently lined with trees that form beautiful tunnels. At the southern end of the trail, there are areas of prairie grasses which served as food for the herds of buffalo and deer that once roamed there. The Wabash Trace is a sanctuary for deer, rabbits, squirrels, wild turkeys, pheasants, quail and score of migratory birds and other animals.

Information

Council Bluffs Parks Dept. (712) 328-4650
Shenandoah Chamber of Commerce (712) 246-3455

County Pottawattamie, Mills, Fremont, Page

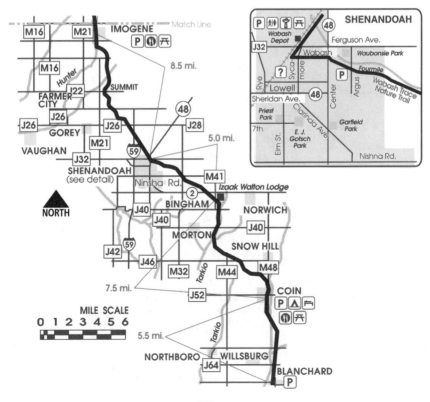

Waubonsie State Park

Trail Length	8.0 miles
Surface	Natural
Vicinity	Sidney
Location & Setting	Southwest corner of the state, near the Missouri River. Sidney is 6 miles north and Hamburg is 9 miles south of the park.
Information	Waubonsie State Park (712) 382-2786
County	Fremont

Fremont County Historical Museum Complex
Multiple-building complex features Indian Room, mastodon tusks, kitchen, living room, bedroom, general store, old drug store fountain from 1863 Penn Drug, toys, clothes, farming equipment, genealogy records. Location East side of square.

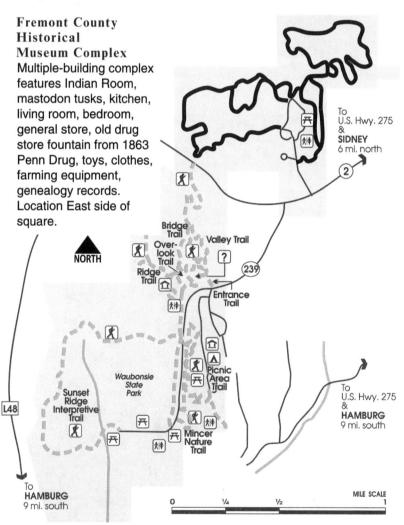

To
U.S. Hwy. 275
&
SIDNEY
6 mi. north

NORTH

Bridge Trail
Over-look Trail
Valley Trail
Ridge Trail
Entrance Trail

Waubonsie State Park

Sunset Ridge Interpretive Trail

Picnic Area Trail

Mincer Nature Trail

To
U.S. Hwy. 275
&
HAMBURG
9 mi. south

To
HAMBURG
9 mi. south

MILE SCALE

0   ¼   ½   1

Waverly Discovery Trail

Trail Length	10.0 miles
Surface	Asphalt
Vicinity	Waverly, Denver
Location & Setting	The Waverly Discovery Trail, with the 2.2 mile City of Denver Trail included, connects the towns of Waverly and Denver in northeast Iowa. Setting is woodland, prairie and some wetland. The route includes eight bridges, and a 500 foot trestle crossing the Cedar River.
Information	City of Waverly (319) 352-6263
County	Bremer

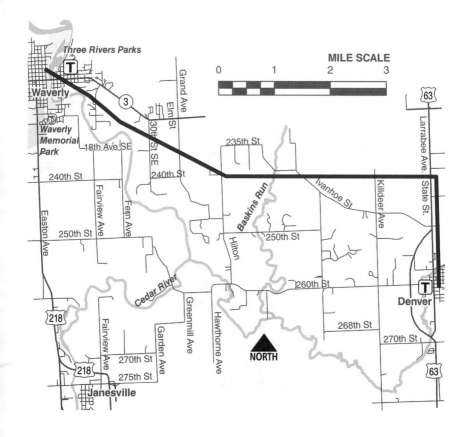

Wilson Island Recreation Area

Trail Length	5.0 miles
Surface	Grassy
Vicinity	Missouri Valley
Location & Setting	The Recreation Area is located about 11-miles southwest of the town of Missouri Valley. It consists of 577-acres of dense cottonwood stand on a level floodplain. The trails are looped and multi-use. There is a Visitors Center. From Hwy 29 & Hwy 30, east of Missouri Valley, south on Hwy 29 for 2-miles to Hwy 362, then west 4-miles to the park entrance.
Information	Wilson Island State Recreation Area (712) 642-2069
County	Pottawattamie

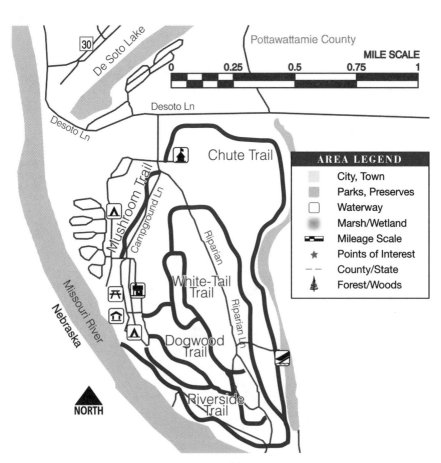

Yellow River State Forest

Trail Length	20.0 miles
Surface	Gravel, grass, dirt
Vicinity	Harpers Ferry, Waukon
Location & Setting	Located in the northeast corner of the state, the biking trail is a segment of abandoned railbed. The forest can be accessed off Hwy. 76 about 10 miles southeast of Waukon or off Hwy. H, 2 miles west of Harpers Ferry.
Information	Yellow River State Forest (319)586-2548
County	Allamakee

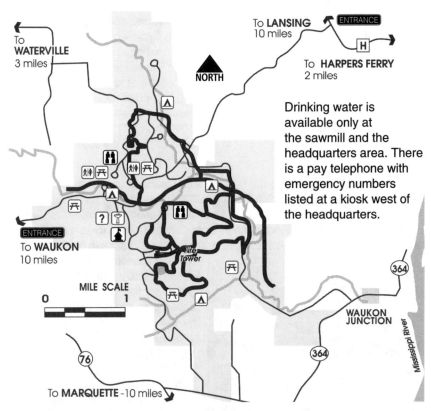

Drinking water is available only at the sawmill and the headquarters area. There is a pay telephone with emergency numbers listed at a kiosk west of the headquarters.

The forest covers some 6500 acres. In addition to the biking trail there are designated hiking and equestrian trails available. There are also fire lanes and logging roads that are not part of the trail system. There are trail logo signs, but, if you become disoriented, get to a road or fence and stay on it and it will eventually lead to help. Be sure to visit Effigy Mounds National Monument which borders the Mississippi River and is not far south on Hwy. 76.

Salt and Pepper Sands of Western Iowa

The modern Missouri River drains a vast area of the American West, with many of its tributaries having headwaters in the Rocky Mountains. The Missouri forms Iowa's western border with Nebraska, and its channel has repeatedly shifted course across the broad north-south valley, which exceeds 15 miles wide in places. Unravelling the geologic evolution of this major valley to its present location has become an important element in the assessment of groundwater resources in western Iowa.

This tooth from a Stegomastodon, a distinctly Pliocene-age member of the ancient elephants, came from gravels at Akron, in Plymouth County, and places the age of this western-derived alluvium at 1.6 to 4.0 million years old (length is 9 inches). *Photo by Tim Kemmis*

Reconstructing the ancestry of the Missouri drainage system involves various lines of geologic evidence. To establish a relative time framework, geologists must investigate the relationships between the various glacial-age deposits that lie above bedrock as well as the evidence of erosional gaps separating them. In general, these deposits consist of a complex sequence of glacial drift left by advances of continental ice sheets from the north at least eight times between about 500,000 and 2.5 million years ago. In addition, rivers deposited large amounts of sand and gravel during melting of these various glaciers as well as during warmer interglacial episodes like today. These buried deposits of sand and gravel are of particular importance to parts of western Iowa as sources of groundwater.

The Geological Survey Bureau initiated a study of these various river deposits in western Iowa during the late 1980's in an effort to understand their distribution, composition, origin, and water-bearing characteristics. Two general types were described: 1) sediments derived from glaciers or glacial deposits to the north and northeast, and 2) sediments resembling those in the modern Missouri and Platte rivers of Nebraska. Included in this latter group are fine-grained sediments called "salt and pepper" sands by well drillers in western Iowa. These sands form a potentially significant source of groundwater across some upland areas where they are commonly buried beneath 50 to 300 feet of glacial deposits. Scattered within the white quartz-rich sand grains are dark "pepper" grains which are identified as fragments of volcanic glass.

The "salt and pepper" sands exposed in a Mills County quarry show angled patterns of cross-bedding which reflect shifting current directions in an ancient river system with headwaters in the Rocky Mountains. *Photo by Greg Ludvigson*

Excerpts from article by Brian J. Witzke
Adapted from Iowa Geology 1991, No.16, Iowa Dept. of Natural Resources

Non-Illustrated Trails Listing

Amana Kolonieweg Rec. Trail

Trail Length	3.2 miles
Surface	Asphalt
Vicinity	Amana
Location & Setting	Located in the Amana Colonies, nationally known as the home of one of America's most successful utopian communities, the trail connects the villages of Amana and Middle Amana. It traverses along the Mill Race Canal, with parking, restroom and concessions available by the Amana Depot trailhead.
Information	Amana Colonies Trails (319) 622- 3639
County	Iowa

Ames City Trails

Trail Length	22.0 miles
Surface	Paved
Vicinity	Ames
Location & Setting	A series of paths throughout the city, with some connecting, and ranging in length from .6 to 2.7 mile. Surface is paved, except for Squaw Creek Path, which consists of screenings. Ames is home to Iowa State University.
Information	Ames Chamber of Commerce (515) 232-2310
County	Story

Cedar View Trail

Trail Length	1.5 miles, plus 3.0 miles of shared roadway
Surface	Crushed limestone
Vicinity	Libertyville
Location & Setting	The trail connects Libertyville with Jefferson County Park. It runs from Hwy 34 to 32nd Street or Hemlock, or Hwy 1 to Libertyville to 32nd Street or 223rd Street.
Information	Jefferson County Conservation Board (641) 472-4421
County	Jefferson

Charles City Trails

Trail Length	5 miles
Surface	Asphalt
Vicinity	Charles City
Location & Setting	The Charles City trail system consists of the 3.5-miles Charles Western Trail and the 1.5-mile Riverside Trail. The Charles Western trail, built on old rail bed, encircles all but the northwest quarter of the city from the White Farm Site to the Wildwood Golf Course. The Riverside Trail travels the north side of the Charles River. Street routes connect the two trails.
Information	Charles City Parks Dept. (641) 257-6312
County	Floyd

City of Denver Trail

Trail Length	4.0 miles
Surface	Crushed stone
Vicinity	Denver
Location & Setting	The trail extends north from the city of Denver and connects with the Waverly Rail Trail at its junction with Hwy 63.
Information	City of Denver
County	Bremer

George Recreation Trail

Trail Length	4.0 miles
Surface	Concrete, asphalt
Vicinity	George
Location & Setting	George is a rural community in northwest Iowa. The trail system encircles the city. There are some street connections. The setting is mostly open, with some sections tree lined.
Information	City of George (712) 475-3512
County	Lyon

Grant Wood Trail

Trail Length	5.3 miles (additional 6 miles planned)
Surface	Turf
Vicinity	Marion, Springville
Location & Setting	This trail is named after the famous artist who lived in Cedar Rapids. It currently runs between Hwy 13 and Springville, and follows the route of the former Milwaukee Railroad. There are plans to extend the trail eastward to Jones County.
Information	Linn County Conservation Board (319) 892-6450
County	Linn

Horseshoe Bend

Trail Length	2.5 miles
Surface	Natural, groomed
Vicinity	Milford
Location & Setting	Located along the Little Sioux River 3.5 miles southwest of Milford in Dickinson County. Setting varies from hilly to flat.
Information	Dickinson County Conservation Board (712) 338-4786
County	Dickinson

Indian Lake Park Trail

Trail Length	4.0 miles
Surface	Crushed stone
Vicinity	Farmington
Location & Setting	Located in the County of Van Buren, near Farmington. An attractive trail area, with accessibility from parking and camping areas within the park.
Information	Van Buren County Conservation Board (319) 293-3589
County	Van Buren

Non-Illustrated Trails Listing (continued)

Lake Manawa State Park 🚲 🚶

Trail Length	4.5 miles
Surface	Paved: 2.5 miles, gravel: 2.0 miles
Vicinity	Council Bluffs
Location & Setting	The paved trail within the park connects to the Western Trails Center, Council Bluffs trail system, and the Wabash Trace Trail. The gravel trail runs on a dike along the shoreline. Facilities include picnic areas, camping, swimming, boating and fishing. The park is located 2.5 miles south of I-80 (Exit 3) at Council Bluffs.
Information	Lake Manawa State Park (712) 366-0220
County	Pottawattamie

Lamoni Recreation Trail 🚲 🛼 🚶

Trail Length	3.2 miles
Surface	Concrete
Vicinity	Lamoni
Location & Setting	This 10-foot wide trail follows the course of the abandoned Burlington and Northern Railway from the Gateway Welcome Center into Lamoni with a loop through Graceland University.
Information	Lamoni City Hall (641) 784-8711
County	Decatur

Little River Scenic Nature Trail 🚲 🛼 🚶

Trail Length	2.0 miles
Surface	Concrete
Vicinity	Leon
Location & Setting	Located in the town of Leon, the trail is built on a former railroad right-of-way. The oak trees planted along the trail provide shade. The trailhead is at N.W. Little River Road and N.W. 7th.
Information	Leon City Hall (641) 446-6221
County	Decatur

Mad Creek Greenbelt

Trail Length	2.0 miles
Surface	Paved, crushed stone
Vicinity	Muscatine
Location & Setting	This is a levy trail, with a Mississippi overlook as part of the trail. Located in the city of Muscatine by Lincoln Blvd., and along Hwy 38 on the north side. There is parking on both ends of the trail.
Information	Muscatine Parks Dept. (563) 263-0241
County	Muscatine

Maple Leaf Pathway

Trail Length	3.0 miles
Surface	Grass, ballast
Vicinity	Diagonal
Location & Setting	Built on former railroad right-of-way, this 3-mile trail has a surface of crushed stone. The trailhead is located in Diagonal, a small community of about 300.
Information	Ringgold County Conservation Board (515) 464-2787
County	Ringgold

Prairie Springs Recreation Area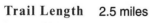

Trail Length	2.5 miles
Surface	Paved
Vicinity	Cresco, Vernon Springs
Location & Setting	This trail runs along the Prairie's Edge Nature Center between Cresco and Vernon Springs. You can access the trail from Cresco at 7th Avenue SW east of Vernon Road, or from the Prairie's Edge nature Center 2 miles south of Cresco on Vernon road.
Information	Howard County Conservation Board (563) 547-3634
County	Howard

Non-Illustrated Trails Listing (continued)

Puddle Jumper Trail

Trail Length	2.3 miles
Surface	Crushed stone
Vicinity	Orange City, Alton
Location & Setting	Located between Orange City and Alton in Sioux County. Setting is open spaces, prairies, and farmland.
Information	Orange City (City Hall) (712) 737-4885
County	Sioux

Ringgold Trailway

Trail Length	3 miles
Surface	Crushed stone, natural-groomed
Vicinity	Mount Ayr
Location & Setting	Located east of Mount Ayr in Ringgold County and built on a former railroad right-of-way. There is a trailhead in Poe Hollow Park, a popular multi-recreational area.
Information	Ringgold County Conservation Board (515) 464-2787
County	Ringgold

Russell White Nature Trail

Trail Length	3.0 miles
Surface	Ballast, Grass
Vicinity	Lanesboro
Location & Setting	This former rail-trail, in west central Iowa, transverses 3 miles of level forest, pastures, and native prairie. It crosses the Raccoon River on a converted 350-foot long trestle.
Information	Carroll County Conservation Board (712) 792-4614
County	Carroll County

Shelby Trail

Trail Length	3.7 miles
Surface	Crushed stone
Vicinity	Shelby
Location & Setting	The town of Shelby is located northeast of Council Bluffs in west central Iowa. The surface is crushed stone. Setting is open. Basic services are available.
Information	City of Shelby
County	Shelby

Sheldon Recreation Trail

Trail Length	3.5 miles
Surface	Paved
Vicinity	Sheldon
Location & Setting	The trail runs along the east side of the city of Sheldon. It continues from Country Club Road, west of the city to the campus for the disabled, across Floyd River.
Information	City of Sheldon
County	O'Brien

Winkel Memorial Trail

Trail Length	10.0 miles
Surface	Crushed stone
Vicinity	Sibley, Allendorf
Location & Setting	The trail runs between Sibley and a mile short of Allendorf with spur to Willow Creek County Recreation Area. It was built on former railroad right-of-way. The Sibley public golf course is adjacent to a portion of the trail.
Information	Osceola County Conservation Board (712) 758-3709
County	Osceola

Winnebago River Trail

Trail Length	3.5 miles
Surface	Crushed stone
Vicinity	Forest City
Location & Setting	Located in Forest City and built on abandoned rail bed. There is an additional 1.8 miles of unimproved trail, and a 1 mile hiking trail. There is an interpretive trail open to fat tire bicycling around the marsh area in Thorpe Park, 5.5 miles west of Forest City.
Information	Winnebago County Conservation Board (641) 565 3390
County	Winnebago

Central Iowa Bike Route

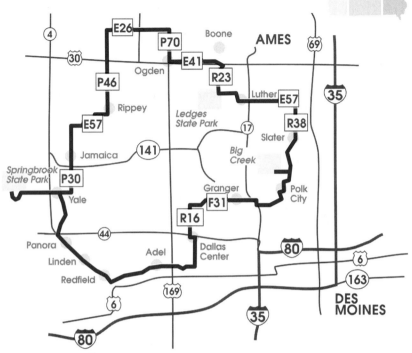

Facilities & Service Available	Restrooms	Food	Restaurants	Drinking Water	Camping	Lodging	Gear Shuttle
Big Creek State Park	•	•		•			•
Slater	•	•	•	•			
Luther	•	•		•			
Ledges State Park	•			•	•		
Boone	•	•	•	•	•	•	•
Ogden	•	•	•	•			
Rippey	•	•		•			
Jamaica	•	•		•			
Yale	•	•		•			
Springbrook State Park	•	•	•				
Panora	•	•	•	•		•	
Linden	•			•			
Redfield	•			•			
Adel	•	•	•	•		•	
Dallas Center	•	•	•	•			•
Granger	•	•		•			
Polk City	•	•	•	•			
Big Creek State Park	•	•		•			•

It is not necessary to ride State Highway 210 to reach Slater. At the intersection of R38 and Highway 210, proceed north .3 miles on gravel. Turn east and ride .5 miles adjacent to the railroad tracks.

The Central Iowa Bike Route connects Big Creek, Ledges and Springbrook State Parks as it ambles through 14 charming towns, both large and small. The route is relatively flat, with a few challenging hills as you make your way across the picturesque valleys of the Des Moines and Raccoon Rivers.

Mileage shown illustrates the Central State Park Bike Route, which is a 160 mile ride in its entirety, starting at Big Creek State Park and ending at Big Creek State Park. Route maybe ridden in either direction.

Mileage	Polk City	Granger	Dallas Center	Adel	Redfield	Linden	Panora	Yale	Springbrook SP	Yale	Jamaica	Rippey	Ogden	Boone	Ledges SP	Luther	Slater	Big Creek SP
Big Creek State Park	4	14	27	35	45	51	57	63	69	75	82	93	118	128	134	139	152	160
Polk City		10	23	31	41	47	53	59	65	71	78	89	114	124	130	135	148	156
Granger			13	21	31	37	43	49	55	61	68	79	104	114	120	125	138	146
Dallas Center				8	18	24	30	36	42	48	55	66	91	101	107	112	125	133
Adel					10	16	22	28	34	40	47	58	83	93	99	104	117	125
Redfield						6	12	18	24	30	37	48	73	83	89	94	107	115
Linden							6	12	18	24	31	42	67	77	83	88	101	109
Panora								6	12	18	25	36	61	71	77	82	95	103
Yale									6	12	19	30	55	65	71	76	89	97
Springbrook State Park										6	13	24	49	59	65	70	83	91
Yale											7	18	43	53	59	64	77	85
Jamaica												11	36	46	52	57	70	78
Rippey													25	35	41	46	59	67
Ogden														10	16	21	34	42
Boone															6	11	24	32
Ledges State Park																5	18	26
Luther																	13	21
Slater																		8

Ledges State Park

Ken Formanek

Photo Courtesy of Iowa Dept. of Natural Resources

You may ride the paved Raccoon Valley Trail between Yale and just west of Adel. A daily trail pass is required and can be purchased at the trailhead.

Detailed directions for the route between Granger and Polk City or Big Creek

Ride east of Granger on F31 (2.5 miles); turn left or north on NW121 (2 miles) at Golf Course Road. Turn right on NW118 which becomes N. Beaver Dr., which becomes NW107; at the T, turn left on 106 for .5 miles; turn left at the cemetery onto 112th and travel across the mile long bridge over Saylorville Lake. After the bridge, you may either take the bike trail to Big Creek or continue on the road to Polk City. To reach Big Creek State Park, ride .25 miles after the bridge. On the right side of the road there is a paved parking lot at the trail access. This trail takes you to Big Creek.

Lake to Lake Bike Route

There are 25 miles of surfaced bike trails within the Cedar Falls/Waterloo metropolitan area and more are planned for completion in the future.

The trail head for the 52 mile Cedar Valley Nature Trail, which connects Cedar Falls/Waterloo with Cedar Rapids, is located on the southeast edge of Waterloo. Trail passes are required for users age 11 and older.

Black Hawk County Conservation Board (319) 266-6813

The Lake to Lake Bike Route connects Pine Lake and George Wyth State Parks, through the Iowa River valley.

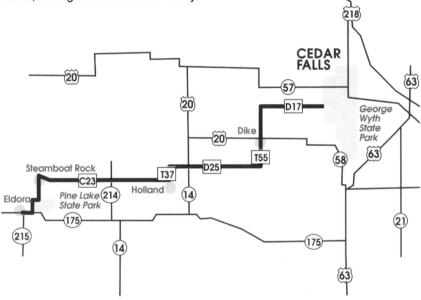

Cold weather shouldn't stop the avid biker. Newly renovated cabins at Pine Lake are open year-round.

Photo Courtesy of Iowa Dept. of Natural Resources

Ken Formanek

Facilities & Service Available	Restrooms	Food	Restaurants	Drink Water	Camping	Lodging	Gear Shuttle
George Wyth State Park	•	•		•	•		•
Cedar Falls/Waterloo	•	•	•	•		•	•
Dike		•	•	•	•		
Holland	•			•	•		
Steamboat Rock	•	•		•			
Pine Lake State Park	•				•	•	•
Eldora	•	•	•	•			•

Gear Shuttle Service

Some bed and breakfasts, motels and park concessionaires offer shuttle service for gear or luggage at a nominal fee. Reservations for this service must be made in advance and some require a minimum number of persons.

Overnight Vehicle Parking

Arrangements must be made in advance to leave your vehicle overnight in any of Iowa's state parks. Park rangers will direct you to the lot designated for over night parking, generally a visitor parking lot adjacent to the campground.

Mileage

Mileage	Cedar F/Waterloo	Dike	Holland	Steamboat Rock	Pine Lake S Park	Eldora
George Wyth State Park	7	18	31	45	49	50
Cedar Falls/Waterloo		11	24	38	42	43
Dike			13	27	31	32
Holland				14	18	19
Steamboat Rock					4	5
Pine Lake State Park						1

Mileage shown illustrates the Lake-to-Lake bike route, which is a 50 mile ride in its entirety, starting at George Wyth State Park and ending at Pine Lake State Park. Route may be ridden in either direction.

Route Clarifications

Holland to Dike: You must back track .5 mile north on Hwy. T37.

Dike to George Wyth State Park through Cedar Falls: Co. Hwy. D17 becomes 27th St.; turn right (or south) on Hudson Rd.; follow Hudson Road to the beginning of Hudson Road Bike Trail which leads to the Green Hill Bike Trail; turn left or east and follow the Green Hill Bike Trail for approximately 6 miles until it crosses the Cedar River to George Wyth State Park; follow the signs to the campground.

North East Iowa Bike Route

The Great River Road has paved shoulders which were designed for bicycle traffic. It is a long winding road along the banks of the scenic and legendary Mississippi River.

Coast down and pedal up the steep hills. This route is designed for the "seasoned" cyclist.

Facilities & Service Available	Restrooms	Food	Restaurants	Drink Water	Camping	Lodging	Gear Shuttle
Wapsipinicon S. Park	•			•	•		
Anamosa	•	•	•	•		•	•
Prairieburg	•			•			
Delhi	•	•	•	•			
Manchester	•	•	•	•		•	
Dundee	•	•		•			
Backbone State Park	•			•	•		•
Petersburg	•	•	•	•			
Colesburg	•	•	•	•			
Osterdock	•	•	•	•			
Guttenburg	•	•	•	•		•	
Pikes Peak State Park		•				•	•
McGregor	•	•	•	•		•	•

Mileage shown illustrates the Northeast Iowa bike route, which is a 130 mile ride in its entirety, starting at Wapsi-pinicon State Park and ending at McGregor. Route may be ridden in either direction.

Mileage	Prairieburg	Delhi	Manchester	Dundee	Backbone S P	Dundee	Petersburg	Colesburg	Osterdock	Guttenberg	Pikes Peak S P	McGregor
Wapsipinicon State Park	19	39	48	60	64	68	66	93	101	108	124	130
Prairieburg		20	29	41	45	49	47	74	82	89	105	111
Delhi			9	21	25	29	47	54	62	69	85	91
Manchester				12	16	20	38	45	53	60	76	82
Dundee					4	8	26	33	41	48	64	70
Backbone State Park						4	22	29	37	44	60	66
Dundee							18	25	33	40	56	62
Petersburg								7	15	22	38	44
Colesburg									8	15	31	37
Osterdock										7	23	29
Guttenberg											16	22
Pikes Peak State Park												6

Route Clarifications

Anamosa E28 can be found by going west of Caseys store on Cherry St.

Prairieburg to Delhi West on E28/X20; north on X20; east on D62; north on X31.

Delhi to Manchester Return to south edge of Delhi to take D5X.

Manchester Will come into town on D5X (Bailey Drive); go west on Main St. which becomes D22.

Dundee to Petersburg NOTE The route jogs on St. Hwy. 38 for .2 mile.

Petersburg to Colesburg NOTE The route jogs east on State Hwy. 3 for .4 mile just before Colesburg.

Guttenberg to Pikes Peak State Park Take X56, the Great River Road, out of Guttenberg.

Pikes Peak State Park to McGregor St. Hwy. 340 does not have paved shoulders.

The North East Iowa Bike Route connects Wapsipinicon, Pikes Peak and Backbone State Parks. Popularly known as the "Little Switzerland" of Iowa, this route is marked by breathtaking bluffs tree topped hills, roller coaster roads and meandering rivers.

South East Iowa Bike Route

This route travels along State Highway 1 for .6 mile from Lacey-Keosauqua State Park to Highway J40. It is possible to ride on the wide gravel shoulder.

The South East Iowa Route

follows along a portion of the Woodland Scenic Byway. Share the roads with the horses and buggies of the Amish residents; enjoy architecture in the National Historic Districts of the villages of Bentonsport and Bonaparte; and in Keosauqua, visit Iowa's oldest county courthouse in continuous use as well as Pearson House, a station on the "underground railroad."

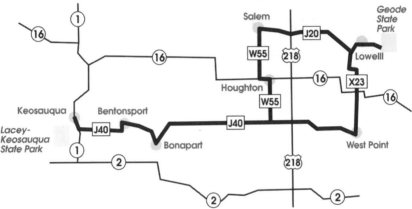

The Forest Craft Festival is held at Lacey-Keosauqua State Park the second weekend of October. It features wood craft demonstrations and sales, forest and wildlife management techniques and colorful buckskinners.

Facilities & Service Available	Restrooms	Food	Restaurants	Drink Water	Camping	Lodging
Keosauqua	•	•	•	•		•
Keosauqua S. Park	•			•	•	
Bentonsport	•	•		•		•
Bonaparte	•	•	•	•		•
Houghton	•	•		•		
Salem	•	•		•		
Lowell						
Geode State Park	•	•		•	•	
West Point	•	•	•	•		

There are many annual celebrations & festivals, including Bike Van Buren, held annually during the third weekend of Aug-ust. The two-day event draws more than 400 bicyclists.

Carry your gear and rough it in the campgrounds or take comfort in a local bed and breakfast or motel along the route.

Mileage	Bentonsport	Bonaparte	Houghton	Salem	Lowell	Geode S. Park	Lowell	West Point	Bonaparte	Bentonsport	Keosauqua SP
Keosauqua State Park	8	12	27	32	42	48	54	63	82	86	93
Bentonsport		4	19	24	34	40	46	55	74	78	85
Bonaparte			15	20	30	36	42	51	70	74	81
Houghton				5	15	21	27	36	55	59	66
Salem					10	16	22	31	50	54	61
Lowell						6	12	21	40	44	51
Geode S. Park							6	15	34	38	46
Lowell								9	28	32	40
West Point									19	23	31
Bonaparte										4	12
Bentonsport											8

Mileage shown illustrates the Southeast Iowa bike route, which is a 93 mile ride in its entirety, starting and ending at Lacey-Keosauqua State Park. Route may be ridden in either direction.

Pedal through scenic splendor

as you explore Iowa's state parks along four bicycle routes, developed to help you enjoy these "places of quiet beauty." Routes primarily travel paved county highways, with an occasional stretch of bicycle trail.

Christine Quinn

SAFETY TIPS
The Lake-To-Lake Bike Route is mostly county highways. Ride on the right side of the road and obey all traffic laws. Be alert at intersections.

Do not create a traffic jam. Ride in double or single file, as traffic dictates.

Wear a helmet. Even a slow fall from a bicycle is enough to create serious injury.

Wear bright colors while bicycling on roadways.

Lake Geode in the summer.
Photo Courtesy of Iowa Dept. of Natural Resources

Trail Index

Trail Index (continued)

City to Trail Index

City to Trail Index (continued)

City to Trail Index (continued)

POPULATION CODES	② 1,000 to 5,000	④ 10,000 to 50,000
① Up to 1,000	③ 5,000 to 10,000	⑤ Over 50,000

County to Trail Index

County to Trail Index (continued)

County to Trail Index (continued)

Explanation of Symbols

SYMBOL LEGEND

- Beach/Swimming
- Bicycle Repair
- Cabin
- Camping
- Canoe Launch
- First Aid
- Food
- Golf Course
- Information
- Lodging
- Multi-Facilities
- Parking
- Picnic
- Ranger Station
- Restrooms
- Shelter
- Trailhead/Access
- Visitor/Nature Center
- Water
- Overlook/Observation

TRAIL USES LEGEND

- Leisure Biking
- Mountain Biking
- Hiking
- Cross-country Skiing
- Horseback Riding
- Rollerblading
- Other

AREA LEGEND

- City, Town
- Parks, Preserves
- Waterway
- Marsh/Wetland
- Mileage Scale
- ★ Points of Interest
- County/State
- Forest/Woods

TRAIL LEGEND

- Bike/Multi Trail
- Hiking only Trail
- XC Skiing only
- Planned Trail
- Alternate Trail
- Road/Highway
- Railroad Tracks

Find me a place, safe and serene,

away from the terror I see on the screen.

A place where my soul can find some peace,

away from the stress and the pressures released.

A corridor of green not far from my home

for fresh air and exercise, quiet will roam.

Summer has smells that tickle my nose

and fall has the leaves that crunch under my toes.

Beware, comes a person we pass in a while

with a wave and hello and a wide friendly smile.

Recreation trails are the place to be,

to find that safe haven of peace and serenity.

By Beverly Moore
Illinois Trails Conservancy

American Bike Trails publishes and distributes maps, books and guides for the bicyclist. For these and other book and map selections visit our website.

American Bike Trails
www.abtrails.com

A Message from the Iowa Trails Council

Have you ever thought about how trails you enjoy came about? Someone first had to *conceive the idea*. Without that thought it would not have happened. After the idea is conceived there is a great deal of labor before the actual *birth* of a trail, with considerable expense involved in the endeavor.

We purchase expensive bicycles, jogging clothes and hiking shoes, skis, snowmobiles and gasoline to get to these trails. Sometimes we pay a fee to help with trail maintenance. Members of the Iowa Trails Council, by their membership, have contributed directly to the *birth and development* of hundreds of miles of trails.

Yes, trees do grow on Iowa's trails
but you know trails do not grow on trees.
Trails are conceived and nurtured by people;
people just like you and me.
No one can build and preserve a major trail all alone.
The ITC needs you and you need us.
Let's conceive and nurture trails in Iowa together.

The Iowa Trails Council is the only trails organization in Iowa devoted exclusively to the acquisition, development and promotion of trails. It is a not for profit organization composed of volunteers. Contributions are used only to create more and better trails and are tax deductible. The Trails Advocate magazine is sent to all members and subscribers.

The Trails State

IOWA TRAILS COUNCIL

The Iowa Trails Council was founded in 1984. Today there are thousands of miles of trails in Iowa's parks and in metropolitan areas. Due largely to the efforts of the Council there are now more than 50 railroad rights-of-way converted in Iowa, amounting to more than 700 miles of rail trails!

Share in this effort by joining and supporting the ITC today.

I wish to contribute to Iowa Trails as a

____ Sponsoring Member	*MORE THAN*	$100
____ Supporting Member		$100
____ Sustaining Member		$50
____ Contributing Member		$25
____ TA Subscriber only		$15

Name _____

Street_____

City _____

State _____Zip_____Tel.# _____

Mail to: **Iowa Trails Council**
Post Office Box 131
Center Point, IA 52213-0131
(319) 849-1844